GLOBAL PRAISE FOR *STRANGE KINGDOM*

"Ken Costa speaks openly of a faith that so many find foolish, and yet has given him the strongest foundation. His honesty opens a window onto the meaning of the cross and the upside-down world it invites us in: a world that has transformed and shaped him, a world he invites us to explore with him. I hope that many readers will take that journey and discover the transforming love of Jesus that lies at its core."

—Justin Welby, Archbishop of Canterbury, England

"*Strange Kingdom* is a joy. It's one of those rare books that uncovers paradigm-shattering insight into an age-old subject. In my forty-seven years in the Christian publishing business, Ken Costa's compelling and inspirational reflections are unique on the meaning and purpose of the cross of Christ. A must-read for every Christian and a revelation for the spiritually curious."

—Joey Paul, Senior Editor, HarperCollins
Christian Publishing, Nashville, Tennessee

"What does the cross of Christ mean for you and me in our everyday lives? At home? In the workplace? In our relationships? In our darkest moments? Through a life of work in the heart of the city of London, our friend Ken Costa has wrestled with these questions. *Strange Kingdom* provides profound wisdom and insight into the most significant events in human history."

—Nicky Gumbel, Vicar of Holy
Trinity Brompton, England

"I love Ken's passion for the Lord Jesus and His finished work at Calvary. May this book inspire and encourage you to receive a fresh revelation of Christ and the power of the cross."

—Joseph Prince, Senior Pastor, New
Creation Church, Singapore

"Ken's approach is so very helpful to people struggling with the relevance of Jesus, the Cross, the Bible in our world today. The power of the cross and the works of Jesus for us today is what *Strange Kingdom* reveals for all of us on the journey towards God in today's world."

—Phil Pringle, Founder and Lead Pastor of
C3 Church, Oxford Falls, Australia

"Ken Costa's deep love for God and unashamed defense of the cross of Jesus Christ is mirrored in this book. The perspective of a banker, the mind of a scholar, and the heart of a Christian who wants people to love Christ radiates on every page. Caution: this book will make you hungry for God and give you the will to be foolish for the weakness of Christ rather than the strength of the world."

—R. T. Kendall, author, teacher, and former
minister of Westminster Chapel, England

"Jesus' final actions secured our forgiveness, split history in half, and started the most powerful movement the world's ever known. My friend Ken Costa masterfully captures the meaning of those final moments in his new book *Strange Kingdom*. It's a brilliant, fresh perspective that shouldn't be missed."

—Steven Furtick, Senior Pastor, Elevation
Church, Charlotte, North Carolina

"This book will encourage your faith and deepen your understanding of what the cross means to people in their day-to-day lives."

—Jentezen Franklin, Senior Pastor, Free Chapel
Worship Center, Gainesville, Georgia

"My friend Ken Costa has written an unprecedented work on the cross of Christ. He blends his daily devotion with deep biblical content and I thoroughly recommend this book to anyone seeking to find out more about the cross of Christ, and what it means to us, in our everyday lives."

—John Gray, Associate Pastor, Lakewood
Church, Houston, Texas

"This book reads like one of the old-time classics and Ken has done a deft job of skillfully weaving the importance of our paying the price into present-day realities."

—Pastor Yang Tuck Yoong, Cornerstone
Community Church, Singapore

"My friend Ken Costa has written a book that will illuminate both your heart and mind with fresh insights on the meaning of the cross, impacting every day of your life, every decision you make, and every date in your diary. A must-read for every believer."

—Pastor Agu, Senior Pastor, Jesus House, England

"Ken Costa has this infectious passion to guide every person he meets to the foot of the cross."

—Steve Carter, Teaching Pastor, Willow Creek
Community Church, South Barrington, Illinois

"Is the cross still important to us today? What is its significance? In his newest book, my good friend Ken Costa masterfully and meticulously gives us an in-depth look at the cross of Jesus and what it means to us in our everyday lives. Filled with relevant and engaging truths, this book will give you a deeper understanding of the value and meaning of the cross."

—Robert Morris, Senior Pastor, Gateway
Church, Southlake, Texas

"My friend and mentor, Ken Costa, understands the human heart and the work of the cross in a way that transcends culture and is as relevant here in Asia as it is in the West. Not since John Stott's *The Cross of Christ* have I read a book on the saving work of Jesus that I want to return to again and again as much as this one."

—Miles Toulmin, Vicar of HTBB,
Kuala Lumpur, Malaysia

"My friend Ken Costa has brilliantly captured the meaning of Jesus' actions in his new book *Strange Kingdom*. I highly recommend it."

—Brett Hilliard, First Pastor,
Island ECC, Hong Kong

"I am convinced this book is going to do what some time spent with Ken always does, grow your love and understanding of the life in Christ we have been invited to."

—Andreas Nielsen, Lead Pastor,
Hillsong, Stockholm, Sweden

"Yes! This book warms my heart. Ken Costa shares both knowledge and fire, both insight and intimacy. It is a Strange Kingdom Jesus launched, but precious all the more. Words are combined with music as worlds collide and Jesus becomes known to the soul searching for him. This is a book to be read slowly, to be pondered deeply, and to be shared widely. May we never forget to celebrate and live the Strange Kingdom in and among us."

—Henk Stoorvogel, Pastor, Free
Evangelization Zwolle, Netherlands

STRANGE KINGDOM

MEDITATIONS ON THE CROSS TO TRANSFORM YOUR DAY-TO-DAY LIFE

KEN COSTA

EMANATE
BOOKS

Published in Nashville, Tennessee, by Emanate Books, an imprint of Thomas Nelson. Emanate Books and Thomas Nelson are registered trademarks of HarperCollins Christian Publishing, Inc.

Thomas Nelson titles may be purchased in bulk for educational, business, fund-raising, or sales promotional use. For information, please e-mail SpecialMarkets@ThomasNelson.com.

Unless otherwise noted, Scripture quotations are taken from the Holy Bible, New International Version®, NIV®. Copyright © 1973, 1978, 1984, 2011 by Biblica, Inc.® Used by permission of Zondervan. All rights reserved worldwide. www.Zondervan.com. The "NIV" and "New International Version" are trademarks registered in the United States Patent and Trademark Office by Biblica, Inc.®

Scripture quotations marked ESV are from the ESV® Bible (The Holy Bible, English Standard Version®). Copyright © 2001 by Crossway, a publishing ministry of Good News Publishers. Used by permission. All rights reserved.

Scripture quotations marked HCSB are from the Holman Christian Standard Bible®. Copyright © 1999, 2000, 2002, 2003, 2009 by Holman Bible Publishers. Used by permission. HCSB® is a federally registered trademark of Holman Bible Publishers.

Scripture quotations marked KJV are from the King James Version. Public domain.

Scripture quotations marked NKJV are from the New King James Version®. © 1982 by Thomas Nelson. Used by permission. All rights reserved.

Scripture quotations marked PAR are paraphrased by Ken Costa.

Any Internet addresses, phone numbers, or company or product information printed in this book are offered as a resource and are not intended in any way to be or to imply an endorsement by Thomas Nelson, nor does Thomas Nelson vouch for the existence, content, or services of these sites, phone numbers, companies, or products beyond the life of this book.

ISBN 978-1-4002-0809-8 (eBook)
ISBN 978-1-4002-0808-1 (TP)

Library of Congress Control Number: 2017961278

Printed in the United States of America
18 19 20 21 22 LSC 10 9 8 7 6 5 4 3 2 1

This book is dedicated to the many Christians who are trying to live out the meaning of the cross in their day-to-day lives. I hope and pray that this book will be of help to you, to live fulfilled and flourishing lives in a broken world.

CONTENTS

INTRODUCTION

"HE LOST, MATE, DIDN'T HE?"

This, the terse response of an atheist friend to the life and death of Jesus Christ. His words hit me as sharply as when I heard the candid indictment by Ted Turner, the founder of CNN: "Christianity is for losers."

Is that what people think Jesus' followers are? Losers?

This refrain has been going round in my head for years. "He lost, mate, didn't he?"

Was the cross a lost cause?

Over time, as I have dug beneath the candid verdict of my friend and the dismissive comments by Ted Turner, I have found myself asking the question: "But did he lose?" I should have challenged his remarks by saying: "It all depends on the battle Jesus was trying to win."

Perhaps my friend and Ted Turner could be forgiven for not understanding the nature of such a battle. The outcome is counter to everything within our contemporary culture and modern vernacular. The death of Jesus, celebrated by Christians as the defining event not only of his life but also of the whole of human history, is a weird concept for a modern mind to grapple with.

There is no denying that during his life Jesus displayed signs of being a remarkable prophet and teacher, and that on the cross he personified and exemplified self-sacrifice. But as for being God—didn't he lose the right to that claim? How could Jesus' death be reconciled with the claims made during his earthly ministry and recorded at the end of Matthew's Gospel that "all authority in heaven and on earth has been given to me?" (28:18).

How can all authority be given to a loser? To someone who was defeated by death? To someone who endured the worst form of capital punishment, reserved only for slaves and rebels? When Jesus shouted with a loud cry, "It is finished," and breathed his last, would it not be preposterous to think that the world had become a different place? That a new era in human history had been inaugurated? To claim that his death and apparent defeat could be disguised as the ultimate victory would be very strange thinking indeed.

> To claim that Jesus' death and apparent defeat could be disguised as the ultimate victory would be very strange thinking indeed.

The modern martyr Dietrich Bonhoeffer witnessed to this strangeness. Bonhoeffer was born into a wealthy and highly cultured German family at the beginning of the twentieth century. After a stellar academic career that led to teaching theology at Berlin University by the age of twenty-five, he was drawn into an organized protest and resistance to the rise of Nazi power. Toward the end of the Second World War, a number of Bonhoeffer's closest friends conceived a plan to assassinate Adolf Hitler. They believed that Bonhoeffer could help them even though he was already in prison for aiding the German resistance movement.

A man of principle, fiercely ethical, and unbending in his commitment to nonviolence, Bonhoeffer initially refused to take part. But, in the end, unable to see any hope for a nation led by Adolf Hitler, he committed himself to a plot to assassinate the führer, even though he believed he was sinning by doing so and would have to face the judgment of God for his actions. In spite of the justness of the cause and the care with which the plot was carried out, the attempt on Hitler's life failed.

Several months later Bonhoeffer was implicated in the plot, tried without witnesses or a defense, and executed by hanging. He died on April 9, 1945, a few short weeks before the suicide of Hitler, the collapse of the Nazi government, and the end of the war. Yet Bonhoeffer's writings from prison demonstrate that he died content and at peace. He had not lived the easy, pleasant life that someone of his gifts and position might have expected. But he had lived a life full of purpose, dedicated to the universal struggle of good against evil, of righteousness against injustice. He had devoted himself to a cause greater than any individual. He understood more deeply than I can imagine what it was like to live as a disciple in the new world-changing age instituted through the death of Christ.

Bonhoeffer had discovered his purpose, understood his struggle, and found the strength to devote himself to a seemingly lost cause through looking to the cross of Christ. By giving his full attention to the meaning and implications of the cross, Bonhoeffer learned that what was truly important was often overlooked and undervalued, causing him to conclude, when meditating on the meaning of the cross: *"A king who dies on the cross must be the king of a rather strange kingdom."*[1]

Bonhoeffer's reflections prompted me to explore the nature of this "strange kingdom." Everything about Jesus' life was counter to the kingdom that his contemporaries were expecting and the empire that Rome had established. Perhaps, therefore, it is not so unusual that the nature of his kingdom would be "strange" to modern-day sensibilities. The man mocked as king is actually King of kings. Strange as it sounds, Jesus' death is his coronation as King and the triumphal beginning of the long-awaited kingdom he preached about.

In light of all this, the primary question whirring round my head is: *What does the cross mean for ordinary Christians, for you and for me, in our everyday lives—at work, at home, in our communities?* Does it have any relevance at all? Was the cross just a mark in human history or a significant shift in the entire story of God's relationship with his creation? Was the cross a stark reminder of a failed prophet with very little to say to a postmodern, performance-driven, technological world? As Brennan Manning said:

> Jesus entered our world as the music man, but the world was disturbed by his song. . . . Jesus wanted to turn the world into a great cathedral organ, and he dug music out of dry bread, herds of pigs, prostitutes, and the dead. Nain, Jericho, Capernaum, and Bethany put two nails into his hands to silence his music.[2]

But did the nails silence the music? Could it be that, in those nails, God succeeded in putting into operation his new creation and plan for the world? Could it be that, in those nails, a new kind of music could be heard?

Whatever our initial answer is to these questions, one of the signs of our times is that addressing the wider world with the

Christian message is strange, difficult, and contentious. And, if we are to do so effectively in this fast-moving digital age, we would be advised by most social commentators not to start by or focus on the meaning of the cross. It is an image so ghoulish and incomprehensible that no person would ever use it as the signature logo for the brand of a new religion, let alone come up with an illogical claim that the cross of Jesus had won the cosmic battle once and for all.

What does the cross mean for ordinary Christians, for you and for me, in our everyday lives—at work, at home, in our communities?

Perhaps, instead, we could attract people by portraying Jesus as a great man whose life was a good example for us, like Ghandi or Mandela. If we were to ask a range of people on the street today what relevance Jesus has in the world, our question would be met with sarcasm and skepticism—or just a blank look. Perhaps they would think him a distant deity detached from the world, part of history and irrelevant. Or perhaps just another failed revolutionary, like the revolutionaries who had gone before, inevitably to be crucified—a task carried out with brutal efficiency by the Romans in ancient antiquity hundreds of times a day. And, as for the resurrection, the contemporary mind just parks it as a fable, a nice story of renewal and new life (along with Easter eggs) but not literally true.

Of course, this opinion reflects a worldview that is deeply embedded within the fabric of our cultural narrative and contemporary discourse. The cross of Christ is seen as a defeat and not a victory. The legacy that matters to the media commentators—if it matters at all—is his teaching and his personal character not his death and certainly not the unbelievable resurrection. Caesar died but we remember him for his great battles. Churchill is remembered for his determination to defeat Hitler. Martin Luther King Jr. is remembered for his dedication to the value of every human being, regardless of skin color and social class. Even Bonhoeffer and the contemporary Christian martyrs in Syria are remembered for their stands against tyranny. So why not Jesus?

There are, however, still many who are captivated by the cross. It is commemorated in every Christian church and is crucial to the life of every Christian. It's the outward visual sign of the Christian faith, a sign of hope for every human being. Even the critics can't ignore it.

I remember the first time I realized the power of the cross. I was a student and had just been told about the liberating way in which Christ had taken my guilt and shame and exchanged it for his peace. None of it seemed to make sense. The cross seemed such a distant and, of course, iconic event but surely of antiquarian rather than contemporary relevance. And yet I knew as it was explained to me that there was a powerful truth affecting me even as I heard the words. I realized that there was a vacuum in the center of my life that could not be filled by any of the many activities of student life. Was there more to life than preparing to be successful?

I knew I was carrying an unexplained but clearly felt weight and burden, a burden of purposeless pursuit of a worldly agenda of prosperity. And then I surrendered my life to Christ and faith came alive. It was a simple prayer, more a cry for help. But in that moment I was set free. In the words of the Wesley hymn: "My chains fell off. My heart was free."[3] There was a sense of liberation in knowing that there was no condemnation now. Shame had gone, guilt had been taken, and I sensed a weight lift from my shoulders—I sensed the presence of God. Something new had started. To this day I can remember where I was in my room at university and the sense of a lightness of heart, as I knew that the cross was the place of encounter with God.

Throughout my career I've tried to draw strength from the reflection of Christ as the one who reached into the darkest place of humankind: death. He faced his death squarely in the eye, and this gives me courage to face the most hostile situations at work, in challenging relationships, and in the fights against injustice both personally and in the world. Even the darkness of depression that hits so many of us does not reach the depth of his suffering. I am secure in the knowledge that I will never have to go anywhere near the darkness he endured. "In your struggle against sin, you have not yet resisted to the point of shedding your blood" (Heb. 12:4). Which leaves us to ask the question: Why does the cross of Jesus matter in our day-to-day lives?

Surely it's irrelevant. Surely we have to just get on with living, rather than focus on a gruesome death? But let us zoom out and take a panoramic picture of the prevailing landscape of our contemporary world. Can't we see in this picture a society that desperately needs God? Love as shown by Jesus, seeking to put others before ourselves and our interests, is a foreign idea to most of our world. And what about our understanding and our definition of love?

> **Even the darkness of depression that hits so many of us does not reach the depth of his suffering.**

At the turn of the millennium, my wife and I went to one of London's greatest tourist attractions, the National Gallery, to an exhibition called "Seeing Salvation," which traced the depiction of Jesus' death from the late classical period to the present day. Most secularists must have wondered why on earth the general public would pay to see old paintings about someone being tortured to death. The foolishness of it! However, people flocked to the National Gallery, which received more revenue during that exhibition than at any other time. It seems that the cross might still have a contemporary appeal if only we could communicate with conviction the power of love to change lives.

This book is a journey of reflection and meditation. It is not a book to be read through in one sitting but rather taken chapter by chapter, perhaps at a significant time in your life. Perhaps in a time of change or when you are seeking a new life challenge or getting back to the simple, radical truth of the good news of the cross of Christ. Each chapter has a meditation to ponder and a suggestion of classical or contemporary music to help in meditation. Of course, it is only a prompt and you will have some of your own songs. There is something powerful in linking worship and the Word.

My prayer is that the puzzle of the power of the cross will draw you into a closer encounter with the risen Jesus Christ.

ONE

FOOLISHNESS

For the message of the cross is foolishness to those who are perishing, but to us who are being saved it is the power of God.

—1 Corinthians 1:18

DAVE EGGERS, BEST KNOWN AS THE AUTHOR OF
A Heartbreaking Work of Staggering Genius (that's his title, not my critical evaluation) has recently published another novel, which touches on big questions of meaning and purpose. In *Your Fathers, Where Are They? And the Prophets, Do They Live Forever?* the central character, Thomas, has kidnapped half a dozen people—including his mother, an astronaut, a congressman, a teacher, a policeman, and the woman of his dreams—and imprisoned them on an abandoned army base overlooking the Pacific Ocean. He does not want them for ransom or revenge but to answer his questions so that he can uncover the meaning and purpose of his life. "Don't we deserve some grand human projects that give us some meaning?" he asks.

Thomas is probably a little unhinged. But he doesn't think himself mad. He believes he's the only person sane enough and brave enough to see the terrible void at the heart of our culture. Thomas has realized that "no one had a plan for anything, [there was no one] very smart at the controls" and has come to believe that his generation is rudderless, with no "righteousness against injustice" worth committing to, no "cause greater than ourselves" to fight for.[1]

The only time religion is discussed, Christianity is dismissed as the most ridiculous and downright pernicious of faiths:

You know how I hate Christianity and all that wretched iconography. You know what? You see pictures of Buddha and he's

3

sitting, reclining, at peace. The Hindus have their twelve-armed elephant god, who also seems so content but not powerless. But leave it to the Christians to have a dead and bloody man nailed to a cross. You walk into a church and you see a helpless man bleeding all over himself—how can we come away hopeful after such a sight? People bring their children to mass and have them stare for two hours at a man hammered to a beam and picked at by crows. How is that elevating?[2]

Of course, Eggers's characters are not original in pointing out that it's a little odd to have a man hanging and dying on a cross as the focal image for a world faith. After all, the anatomy of kingdom administrations down through the ages has always operated quite differently from Jesus' kingdom regime. Usually a kingdom consisted of one person at the helm leading the charge. That person held a certain pattern or set of values, using imperial power as the vehicle to help bring these values about, which led to victory. Broadly, that was how it worked. A king was powerful, and his subjects lived in awe and respect of his power and majesty.

I recall a visit my wife and I made to Morocco to celebrate one of my birthdays. We went to an oasis in the desert, far away from the markets of Marrakech or the casbahs of Casablanca. As we tried to get to the airport to continue our journey, we were told that all the roads had been closed, but we were not given a reason. The police were out in force, as were the military. We also noticed that, in this very remote part of the country where we were staying, there were flags flying from houses and pennants from television aerials. A general sense of celebration in the air seemed to produce smiles on everyone's faces, even if we couldn't fathom what was going on. English only goes so far! Finally, stranded in the village and unable to go anywhere else, we met a young Moroccan who conveyed to us in halting English the reason for this interruption of daily life: the king was coming! He had not been seen in the flesh for a decade, but his power and authority went before him, and each citizen responded as would be expected to the arrival not of a politician or even a celebrity, but of a king.

Generally speaking, through the ages, we have looked at power through the lens of strength, brute force even. Yet Jesus' definition of power, in the strange kingdom he inaugurates on earth, is something new and perhaps shocking—a genuine alternative to the political power constructs of this world.

Jesus' followers have always had to lay down the viewpoints of their era. And I want us to dare to lay down our default settings and twenty-first-century perspectives and delve into the apparently foolish nature of God. The glory of God's wisdom is hidden from the powers of the world (1 Cor. 2:6–7). And the symbol of the cross hangs over the world in its distorted, twisted imagery of pain and shame, not as a worldly power story, but as a story of love. It offers a different kind of truth, not brittle and fragile, but supple and strong and capable of taking on the world in quite a different way.

> Jesus' definition of power, in the strange kingdom he inaugurates on earth, is something new and perhaps shocking—a genuine alternative to the political power constructs of this world.

The Christian story is all about God dying on a cross, in the shadows, at the wrong end of the Roman empire. It's all about God appearing to babble nonsense to a room full of philosophers. It's all about the true God confronting the world of power and over-throwing it in order to set up his own strange kingdom, a kingdom in which the weak and the poor, the foolish and the marginalized find themselves just as accepted as the strong and the wise. It's all about a change that came from below, rather than being imposed from above. We must, then, explore further the foolishness of this strange kingdom, in the hope that we may, paradoxically, gain godly wisdom.

My passion for understanding the person of Jesus has grown dramatically over the years, with an ever-increasing desire to know him more. This has encouraged me to explore the extraordinary and apparently "foolish" nature of this unlikely king and why this strange kingdom he established should have any meaning in the modern world. How has an upside-down kingdom turned the world inside out?

Jesus' Earthly Life

First, we see this apparent foolishness being present in Jesus' life. His earthly life, as far as we can tell, was uneventful. He was born Jewish, in the small town of Bethlehem. Jesus arrived in the stench of an old stable. Rather than royal red carpets, there was a dirty floor covered in hay and manure, and most likely a family of mice. The hallowed presence of God turned up at the time that Bethlehem was a vassal state and political backwater on the fringe of the Roman Empire. From the very beginning, in the place he was born, to the very end, in the way in which he

How has an upside-down kingdom turned the world inside out?

died, it was through the lens of utter weakness and helplessness that we would witness and see God's love break into the world.

What utter foolishness. The entire scene is underlain with the resounding message that complete weakness and dependency will always be the occasion for God to exert his power. Such a view is foolishness to those whose idea of a king is defined by the world-view of the powerful.

Jesus grew up in a village alongside brothers, sisters, extended family, and friends. He learned a trade and labored in Galilee, a rural northern region whose inhabitants were considered rude and uncultured by the more sophisticated city dwellers. In the stories of his life we see someone fully human as though he was not God, and fully God as though he was not human. Jesus seemed startlingly uninhibited by social convention or religious rules, by his peers' expectations, or even by the natural laws of the universe. He refused to observe the Sabbath as the religious authorities would have liked. He dined with prostitutes and tax collectors. He preached a message of radical inclusivity in which neighborliness is defined not by color, creed, or familial inheritance, but by an outrageous, sacrificial love.

The secrets of this strange kingdom work in upside-down, unlikely, foolish ways because the God we meet in Jesus is unlike anything or anyone we've ever known. Jesus spoke of God not as a Lord but as a father. And Jesus spoke of himself as a son. He told the outcast that their sins were forgiven, but the so-called righteous that they would be condemned. He proclaimed that the kingdom of heaven is coming, but refused to lift a hand against the Roman occupation. He was a homeless wanderer without a roof to call his own, and yet he spoke as if all the world belonged to him. And while he got angry at the presence of moneylenders in the temple court, he claimed for himself an affinity with God that goes beyond blasphemy.

He is a mass of contradictions and paradox, and yet he strikes me, even from the distance of two thousand years, as someone deeply compelling. Ever since that day in my room at university when I first encountered the Gospel stories, I have been mesmerized by the person of Jesus and the foolish nature of his power, and I remain so to this day.

The secrets of this strange kingdom work in upside-down, unlikely, foolish ways because the God we meet in Jesus is unlike anything or anyone we've ever known.

Jesus didn't command legions or amass millions of loyal followers. He was seen as a religious rebel with a ragtag bunch. If his humble life wasn't enough to illustrate the absurdity of his magisterial claims, his death was surely proof. There he was, nailed to a wooden beam, bloodied and naked, abandoned by his friends. Scorned by the mob and jeered by the soldiers he forgave. Dying in agony, and run through with a spear just to make sure he was dead. This isn't what a Messiah or a king looks like. This certainly isn't what God looks like. Even his most loyal followers lost hope and disowned him. Their dreams of a new kingdom were now dashed to pieces on the rocky outcrop of Golgotha, where foolishness was epitomized and the wisdom of Rome once again made its mark for all to see.

Furthermore, the Gospels reveal Jesus was Lord over creation: fish swam into nets at his command; he walked on water and calmed the storms with a word. He healed the sick, the deaf, the blind, the lepers, and the disabled. No form of sickness was outside his powerful, creative, and regenerative love. He was the Lord over the demonic. Those held in the vise of Satan were set free with just a word from Jesus; the demons knew they were dealing with the Son of God.

Yet, despite being Lord of all, Jesus didn't usher in an aggressive kingdom regime reminiscent of Roman rule, but a kingdom to be inherited by the poor, the meek, the grieving, and the broken. In other religions people reached after God, but in our foolish story God reached out for us. Humility and apparent foolishness are the doorposts into this seemingly strange kingdom of God.

At every point his very ordinariness seemed extraordinary. He went through life one day at a time, one meal at a time, just like his contemporaries, but he never seemed rushed, never appeared out of control, never lacked time for the people who approached him. Jesus would constantly get out of his own skin and place himself in the midst of someone else's story. Jesus didn't see the outcasts as irredeemable; he saw them as invaluable and irreplaceable—not outcasts, but offspring who could be adopted into his family.

Was it foolish for the Son of God to choose to submit to the political and imperial powers of his day? Was it foolish to forgo coronation before crucifixion? To suffer as a criminal when he could have been crowned king? Powerful regimes usually change people from the outside in; but Jesus' influence changed people from the inside out.

The theme of Jesus' earthly life is one of flipping the expectations of the world on their heads—and this theme continues to the end. When Jesus was lured into danger by the deceit of a

> **Powerful regimes usually change people from the outside in; but Jesus' influence changed people from the inside out.**

friend and arrested on false charges by men who were jealous of his influence, he looked with love upon the traitor and healed those who came with swords and clubs to imprison him.

It had become the most polarizing week in the history of humanity. But it was a week that had started with the sound of timbrels, and with children shouting "Hosanna!" and putting palm branches at his feet. They greeted him as a king, but by the end of the week he had been cast out. The book of Luke makes it apparent that this is what true power looks like. This is what it looks like when the promises of Scripture are fulfilled and Israel's Messiah returns at last to his people. He will not come in a blazing fire, or in a pillar of cloud and fire, but as a young prophet, weak and vulnerable, riding into the city on a donkey (Luke 19:28–41).

His trial was a travesty of justice, yet he refused to plead his innocence—and his silence was majestic. How foolish, we think, not to defend himself. But what seemed like silence was really a pregnant pause as Jesus prepared to birth a new kingdom on the other side of his death.

When Jesus eventually died—nailed to a beam, hanging on a cross outside of Jerusalem—it was at the time of the Passover. But there was nothing particularly unusual about that. The great festivals were often times of unrest and insurrection, making the Romans jumpy and overzealous in their punishments. This death, however, was different. This crucifixion ushered in a new creation, a new world that would be celebrated on the first Easter Sunday.

As the onlookers mocked him and called him "king of the Jews," we remember his dialogue with Pilate. Jesus did claim that he was the king of a kingdom, but he said that this was a very strange kingdom, one for which the world had no grid, no reference, no framework. Jesus said, "My kingdom is not of this world. If it were, my servants would fight to prevent my arrest by the Jewish leaders. But now my kingdom is from another place" (John 18:36).

All these glimmers of the extraordinary, in the midst of the ordinary, mark this man, this Jesus, as utterly unique among the handful of miracle workers who crisscrossed Israel. Unique among the rural laborers who plied their trades in Galilee. Unique among the many who were tortured and killed by the Romans. Unique, in fact, among the millions who populated the Roman Empire. Unique, indeed, among all the billions of humans who have ever lived. It was precisely the strange meshing of the ordinary and the extraordinary that proclaimed his uniqueness. It was God's ability to use small, seemingly insignificant encounters to set the stage for significant impact. With every strike of the hammer, it looked as if the dark would win. But it was God's masterstroke.

This isn't what a Messiah looks like. This certainly isn't what God looks like. Even his most loyal followers lost hope and disowned him, their dreams of a new kingdom dashed to pieces on the hill of Golgotha. And yet. And yet. Somehow this was not the end. On the day after Jesus' death, it looked as if whatever small impact Jesus left on the world and his followers would shortly disappear. Instead, his impact on human history is beyond measure.

Of all the extraordinary miracles of this extraordinary rabbi, he saved the best for last. He returned. He appeared. The great stone that covered his tomb was rolled back, and he encountered one of his most devoted disciples, a woman named Mary. He sent her to the others with a message: "I am ascending to my Father and your Father, to my God and your God" (John 20:17). Even here, Jesus turned earthly convention on its head.

The first apostle, the first messenger of the greatest hope

the world has ever known, was a woman. Not just any woman either, but a woman who, if tradition is to be believed, had once earned her keep through prostitution. Because of her status, Mary couldn't even testify in a court of law. By earthly standards she was a foolish choice to carry the message of the risen Messiah. Wild-eyed in her determination to tell the story, she was barely able to contain her excitement and stumbled over her words in a rush to get them out. What a fool she must have looked; that is, until Jesus turned up himself, and her foolishness was vindicated. And the disciples started to believe, once again, that their Jesus, their *rabboni,* was the Messiah. Is the Savior. Is God. Someone without beauty or majesty or attraction, but who would nevertheless flip the world upside down, turning weakness and pain into strength and healing.

This is the suffering servant Isaiah prophesied about:

> He had no beauty or majesty to attract us to him,
>> nothing in his appearance that we should desire him.
> He was despised and rejected by mankind,
>> a man of suffering, and familiar with pain.
> Like one from whom people hide their faces
>> he was despised, and we held him in low esteem.
>
> (Isa. 53:2–3)

The Foolishness of God

The apostle Paul wrote, "Although they claimed to be wise, they became fools" (Rom. 1:22).

Doesn't that just say it all? It's not as simple as saying that the message of the cross is foolishness, as if we should be ashamed of it. This is the foolishness *of God*—a foolishness that shames human wisdom. To those who can understand, the foolishness of God is not the end of wisdom. On the contrary, said Paul, it is "wiser than human wisdom" (1 Cor. 1:25). It is true wisdom. The true order of things. The pulse and heartbeat at the center of all that exists. The soil out of which everything lasting and permanent grows. True wisdom is God's opinion on the matter, the presence of the mind of Christ in every situation.

To the wisecrackers setting off philosophical fireworks, to the bestselling author parked comfortably on TV chat room sofas, to the self-proclaimed gurus of lifestyle and food and choices and moral mazes, the Bible says, this is not wisdom. All power and pomp, blings, rings, and things will eventually turn into shackles. God's wisdom is way above all this. So much so that it is, in fact, human wisdom that is foolish. And those who do believe, those whom the world deems foolish, are given the power of God.

We might well ask why God didn't choose a more obvious, a more powerful, a more comprehensible manifestation on earth. Wouldn't that have been simpler and more effective? What was wrong with an earthly king? Why not come in a form capable of commanding the respect of the nations?

The Symbol of the Cross

We also might wonder why we focus so much on the travesty of the cross. The thought-world of early Christianity had other symbols in use less offensive than the cross: the peacock whose flesh was thought not to decompose even in death; the pelican, who would pluck at her own breast and feed the chicks on her own flesh; Jesus the shepherd, who keeps his flock safe; Jesus the warrior, who stormed the gates of hell. All legitimate. All powerful. Yet by the early third century it was becoming clear that it was this striking, paradoxical image of the cross that was gripping the Christian community. The church leader and theologian Tertullian wrote of the "devotees of the cross" and of the "sign of the cross."[3]

For the last two thousand years, the most powerful image of divinity the world has ever known has been a political prisoner, dying the death of a common criminal. You cannot reason this into coherence. It is foolishness to try. The strangeness is a part of the story we cannot eliminate. We are talking of matters far beyond human understanding, of the divine packaged up in human form. It's like a two-dimensional shape trying to make sense of something in three dimensions. We shouldn't be surprised that our finite brains and limited minds struggle to comprehend the ways and means of God.

What we can do is travel together on a journey that takes us toward a deeper and more life-changing understanding of the cross. And Paul promised those who are being saved, those who put their trust in Jesus Christ, that the cross is the very power of God made real in our lives. That's the heart of it—a strange king, a strange kingdom, foolishness to outsiders, yet of immense potency to those with eyes to see, ears to hear, and hearts open to the Spirit.

The cross is the very power of God made real in our lives.

As Paul explained in his letter to the Corinthians, God chose the foolish things of the world to shame the wise; God chose the weak things of the world to shame the strong.

He chose the lowly and despised things of the world, and the things that are not, to nullify the things that are. It is no surprise that those who complacently trust in their own strength, their own intellect, their own good sense cannot receive the power released by Jesus' death on a cross. Those who are wise in their own eyes, who philosophize from their armchairs, who fill web forums, comment sections, vlogs, blogs, and chat rooms with their opinions mistake the strangeness for nonsense.

The cross defeats the very method and motives that the world prides itself on. To put it another way: the cross demonstrates the powerful foolishness that is of God and beats the foolish powers and regimes of the world. Game over. Jesus won.

The cross may have looked like losing, but it was winning. The cross still looks to many as though the authorities and powers successfully disarmed Jesus and won the battle. But if, in fact, it was the other way round, if this strange kingdom was established by seemingly foolish means, how does it impact our lives?

A Cruciform Kingdom

The cross of Christ is the foundation of God's kingdom—a cruciform kingdom ruled by the "Lamb who was slain."

> Then I saw a Lamb, looking as if it had been slain, standing at the center of the throne, encircled by the four living creatures and the elders. . . . the four living creatures and the twenty-four elders fell down before the Lamb. Each one had a harp and they were holding golden bowls full of incense, which are the prayers of God's people. And they sang a new song, saying:

"You are worthy to take the scroll
    and to open its seals
because you were slain,
    and with your blood you purchased for God
    persons from every tribe and language and people and nation.
You have made them to be a kingdom and priests to serve our God,
    and they will reign on the earth."

Then I looked and heard the voice of many angels, numbering thousands upon thousands, and ten thousand times ten thousand. They encircled the throne and the living creatures and the elders. In a loud voice they were saying:

"Worthy is the Lamb, who was slain,
    to receive power and wealth and wisdom and strength
    and honor and glory and praise!"

(Rev. 5:6–12)

Every enemy of Jesus is now sitting under his feet (Eph. 1:22), and Jesus is seated at the right hand of his Father in heaven (Mark 16:19). This could only be achieved because Jesus obediently and willingly went to the cross and won the ultimate victory. Every benefit Jesus now has available to him only makes sense and remains a consequence of the cross.

This, the cruciform shape of the kingdom, has huge implications for you and me. When faced with our daily struggles and challenges, when it looks as though everything is chaotic and out of control, we can remain confident, knowing that the cross-shaped kingdom is founded upon grace. And "grace means God's love in action toward people who merited the opposite of love."[4]

Jesus could have chosen brute political power, but he chose love. And we have the same choice to make. Will we live by the premises of the world or by the promises of his Word? Will we live by love, which chooses to sacrifice, to forgive, and to submit to God's ultimate power? Or will we grasp power for ourselves, so we can protect our own interests?

Will we live by the premises of the world or by the promises of his Word?

Indeed, this choice—whether to live by the premises of the world or the promises of God—is found in Peter's correspondence to the Christian community. The church was baffled because it was being persecuted so severely. They were followers of Jesus, they reasoned, so surely they should not be suffering. Yet Peter wrote to them, assuring them that this is the shape of the cruciform kingdom, and this is the means by which Jesus was bringing his kingdom to earth: serving amid hostility, suffering injustice, experiencing persecution, choosing to love.

Peter bid them remember that the premises of the world will fade, but the promises of God will live forever. He wrote:

> For you have been born again, not of perishable seed, but of imperishable, through the living and enduring word of God. For,

> > "All people are like grass,
> >   and all their glory is like the flowers of the field;
> > the grass withers and the flowers fall,
> >   but the word of the Lord endures forever."

> > (1 Peter 1:23–25)

Taking Up Our Cross

Therefore, we who have been united to the resurrected Jesus and who, by the power of his Holy Spirit, are living by his promises have been swept into the story of this strange kingdom. And his greatest promise to us is that we will have life in all its fullness (John 10:10). We have to decide whether we will trust his promises and bear witness to this kingdom by taking up our own cross, by embracing its foolishness in the eyes of modern sensibilities, and by choosing love over power. Greatness in this kingdom is characterized by the apparent foolishness of surrender, service, and sacrifice. Jesus said, "Whoever wants to be my disciple must deny themselves and take up their cross daily and follow me" (Luke 9:23).

Taking up our cross will make us live differently, make decisions differently, conduct our relationships differently. The wisdom of the world (exemplified by power) and the wisdom of God (exemplified by love and sacrifice) stand distinct and apart. And we must choose which we will rely upon, which will carry more weight in our lives.

We tend to rely far too much on worldly wisdom and circumstantial evidence, letting our circumstances dictate how we feel and act, shaping what we believe. When we let worldly wisdom creep in, there is a smokescreen of doubt between ourselves and God. Faith is relying on the direct evidence of Scripture. It doesn't mean you deny reality; it simply means you're in touch with a greater reality—a reality that is far more real than the reality you can touch or taste or see or hear or smell.

On the cross, we might say that God created a new ecosystem: an ecosystem built on self-giving, an ecosystem that chose self-giving love over self-serving power. In fact, we might say that the power of this ecosystem is the love the Father showed to the Son, and the Son showed to us by dying on a cross. In this strange kingdom, love has become power.

This is a type of love that cannot be fully understood in a human context: a love that is relentless, persistent, utterly unconditional. "God so loved the world, that he gave his only begotten Son, that whosoever believeth in him should not perish, but have everlasting life" (John 3:16 KJV).

God created a new ecosystem: an ecosystem built on self-giving, an ecosystem that chose self-giving love over self-serving power.

The word *whosoever* is extraordinary. Christ ascended to the stage of heaven, but he lives his moments now within the stairwell of every human heart. When we give generously to someone, we rather hope to see it appreciated and acknowledged. Our system of love is based on reciprocity, for the main part. It is how marriages, friendships, and healthy relationships work. But God's love for us is bigger, wilder, and more incomprehensible than we can imagine. It is *agape* love, not filial love. It is love for the loveless, love for the "whosoever." It is a flood of love even if nothing is returned, not even a nod of acknowledgment.

God's love has no bounds. When we are facing a time of transition—a new career path, for example, or starting a family—we can know that God is faithful and unchanging. He, too, has faced times of change: as he grew up from child to adult, as he left Nazareth to begin his ministry, as he entered Jerusalem to die. In the frailty of our humanity, we can know that God has been weak as a babe, yet he is our strength.

In the darkness of depression, we can know that every situation we face, every dark night of despair we feel, is understood by the God who experienced darkness. Because he conquered darkness by rising from the dead, he is our hope and gives us hope not only for life but for life after the grave. Because only in and through Jesus Christ are we fully known and fully loved, our motives revealed, yet we are never rejected.

The Divine Mosaic

Of course, anyone who looks at the cross as a single screenshot on the monitor of their mind will think God is not loving or powerful but cruel and unfeeling. But when we see the cross as a part of the whole story, we will see it as a shining tile in the divine mosaic that is the story of God. In a rapidly changing world, we can look to the God who navigated the social and political complexities of his time, yet is our constant. We can know that God is not waiting for us on the other side of suffering. He understands its significance and meets us in the midst of our suffering. We may never know why God allows suffering, but we know that God allows his heart to break as we suffer.

To those who do believe, to those who embrace the foolishness, Jesus opens up a new reality, a new dimension, a reality that transforms the poverty of our nature by the riches of his grace. In Jesus, we find a way of living that decries the cycles of vengeance, the constant self-promotion, and the search for supremacy that so frequently characterize human relationships. In him we find a path to the peace and contentment that all are searching for but few will find.

It is in this strange kingdom that we find grace that lays its arm down a wooden beam and never stops reaching out, reaching for you and for me, reaching straight across walls and through fences to bring us eternal life. It is in this strange kingdom that we can live knowing that the remaking of everything has already begun. It is through this strange kingdom that Jesus turned everything over. As N. T. Wright said, "We are to be the upside-down people, or rather the right-way-up people, whose lives from God in Christ are a cheerful standing question mark, challenge, rebuke, warning and invitation to the rest of the world."[5]

Our faith and our calling do not rest in human wisdom, but in the power of God. This means we must pray daily for this kingdom to come on earth as it is in heaven. It is an invitation for us to take up our cross, the apparent foolishness of it and the scorn that may come because of it, and confront the world's foolish power with the fact there is a different way of wielding power. The world longs for a real and radical alternative.

A mocking sign stood above the bloodied body of a man who was suffocating to death: The King of the Jews. What sort of foolish king and what sort of foolish kingdom was this? One where the crown was made of thorns, a sign of apparent curse and defeat. But the thorns symbolize for us the ultimate sacrifice of himself, which was the ultimate declaration of his love.

It is time to stop being

It is time to stop being compelled by the world's foolish power and instead to embrace, whatever it may cost our personal convenience and comfort, the powerful foolishness that is found in the cross of Jesus Christ, King of kings.

compelled by the world's foolish power and instead to embrace, whatever it may cost our personal convenience and comfort, the powerful foolishness that is found in the cross of Jesus Christ, King of kings. Followers of such a King, we form a strange community. The ladder of grace reaches down. To you and to me.

The founder of Apple's closing words in his commencement address to the young people at Stanford University were, "Stay hungry! Stay foolish." Decoded for Christians, these words remain powerful to shape our lives. Stay hungry for God and be foolish when it comes to accepting the weakness of Christ rather than strength of the world.

A Time to Meditate

Music

- "Man of Sorrows," Hillsong
- "Agnus Dei," Samuel Barber

Reflect

- Jesus was born in the stench of an old stable. Can you picture the scene? He dined with prostitutes and tax collectors. Can you picture the scandal? He preached a message of radical inclusivity. Have you made his reach too small? We're called to take Jesus with us. Everywhere. To everyone.

- We look at the cross and what looks like losing is win-ning. Jesus could have chosen earthly power. But he chose divine love. Earthly power is the wisdom of the world, and we are not immune to its appeal. But love is the wisdom of God, and it will never fail us. Which will you choose to live by? Earthly power or divine love?
- Steve Jobs' closing words in his address to the young people at Stanford University were, "Stay hungry! Stay foolish." May you stay hungry and you will be fed. In abundance. And may you stay foolish. May your life be a question mark to those around you. And may all your answers be grace.

Prayer

Lord, thank you that there is nowhere and no one beyond the reach of your love. I ask that you would empower me to resist the wisdom of the world and to live for you and for others by the foolishness of the cross, amen.

TWO

FORSAKEN

At noon, darkness came over the whole land until three in the afternoon. And at three in the afternoon Jesus cried out in a loud voice, *"Eloi, Eloi, lema sabachthani?"* (which means "My God, my God, why have you forsaken me?"). When some of those standing near heard this, they said, "Listen, he's calling Elijah." Someone ran, filled a sponge with wine vinegar, put it on a staff, and offered it to Jesus to drink. "Now leave him alone. Let's see if Elijah comes to take him down," he said. With a loud cry, Jesus breathed his last. The curtain of the temple was torn in two from top to bottom. And when the centurion, who stood there in front of Jesus, saw how he died, he said, "Surely this man was the Son of God!"

—Mark 15:33–39

WE WOULD DO WELL TO CONSIDER JUST HOW
devastating that experience of separation must have been for Jesus.
We have perhaps witnessed harrowing scenes in a documentary
or film where children are separated from their parents, either by
force or by uncontrollable circumstances. I recently read the book
Lion, which became an Oscar-winning film. It tells the harrowing
story of a young Indian boy, aged five, becoming separated from
his older brother at a train station and getting lost. He boards a sta-
tionary train in an attempt to find his brother, and when the doors
slam shut behind him, he begins a journey across the breadth of
India, all the way to Calcutta. The separation from his mother and
his siblings is heart-wrenching and couldn't fail to move even the
steeliest reader. The helplessness, the isolation, the sense of being
so cruelly ripped out from the safety and security of his loving
family—it all hits you in the stomach.

It is hard for us to conceive a separation worse than that of a
young child from a parent, but that's exactly what we see at the cross.
"My God, my God, why have you forsaken me?" is one of the most
remarkable questions in the history of humanity. It has always been
one of the most difficult of all Jesus' sayings for me to understand. It
not only gives us a glimpse into the emotional dimension of his suffering, but also the relational dynamic at the cross. Jesus has *become*
sin—as he chooses to identify 100 percent with the wrongs of all
humanity across all time—and the perfect relationship between the
Father and Son that existed before all eternity is put under the most

extreme pressure. In fact, this is the only time in the Gospels when Jesus prays to God and doesn't use the word *Father*.

> "My God, my God, why have you forsaken me?" is one of the most remarkable questions in the history of humanity.

The sky went dark from the sixth hour, twelve midday, until the ninth hour. Three hours of darkness. The darkness that lay over Golgotha both symbolized and portrayed what was going on in Jesus' spirit. The Son of God felt as if the sun of God's favor had been eclipsed by the sin of the entire world. In the Bible, a darkening sky is indicative of God's judgment. Many years before, Amos had prophesied these words from the Lord's mouth: "I will make the sun go down at noon and darken the earth in broad daylight. . . . I will make that time like mourning for an only son" (Amos 8:9–10). God darkened the sun, and God in Christ took the judgment on himself.

A Series of Substitutions

In this moment, Jesus is forsaken, so that all who have sinned and fallen short of the glory of God might be forgiven. God substitutes himself for humanity. He takes what we deserve. And a whole series of substitutions follow. God's wisdom, as we saw in chapter 1, is revealed in apparent foolishness. God's victory is revealed in defeat. God's power is shown in weakness. God's blessing is hidden in a perceived curse. His love is found in judgment, and his faithfulness in forsakenness. Jesus died so that humanity might live. He suffered so that we might be saved. And by refusing to repay the wrongs done to him, he broke the pattern of tit for tat, eye for eye, tooth for a tooth—the revenge and recrimination that would spiral infinitely onward. He stopped it in its tracks. He crucified our sin by nailing it to the cross.

It is here at Calvary's cross that Jesus broke the chain of sin, broke the curse of death, and broke the code of our disobedient nature by being himself obedient, even under the threat of death, and so opening the way for all people to live in obedience to God. He shattered the determinist worldview that says there is no escape from our natural selves, our self-referential attitudes, our fear, our mean spirits, and our concomitant shame.

The sinless Son of God took the blame and took the hit for sinners. Jesus had been lovingly connected to his heavenly Father throughout eternity, from before the foundation of the world, and now this connection was, in some sense, suspended. Yet the poignancy of this cry of despair, the only one of the sayings of Jesus on the cross that is recorded in Mark's Gospel, reverberates down the ages as a cause of shock and confusion because Christians believe that Jesus actually *is* God.

So how could he be forsaken by God? Is God the kind of God that turns his back on his Son? Does God abandon those who cry out to him? If God could forsake the only one who loved him perfectly and served him with his whole heart, isn't it possible God could forsake us? How can we trust him?

Abandoned

How could the Word made flesh be inflicted with such wounds? Where is God in Jesus' emotional pain? The three divine persons of the Father and the Son and the Holy Spirit are united at such a fundamental level that it is entirely appropriate and correct to describe these three persons as the *one* God. Tim Keller wrote, "God is not more fundamentally one than he is three, and he is not more fundamentally three than he is one."[1] This is the doctrine of the Trinity in a nutshell. So how could Jesus be God-forsaken any more than you or I could be self-forsaken?

Is it possible that the perfect, harmonious unity of the Trinity— the persons within God who exalt one another, commune with one another, and defer to one another—could be fragmented and broken on that cataclysmic day, at three in the afternoon, two thousand years ago? After all, the greatest pain Jesus had to endure was not the whips or the crown of thorns, not the mocking and vitriol that came out of the mouths of his persecutors, not even the excruciating agony of the nails and asphyxiation. As horrendous as all of that was, the worst part was to be separated from his Father. So why did it happen?

Let us look more closely at Jesus' state of abandonment as a way of answering these crucial questions. The word *godforsaken* is often used as a way to describe a very distant, inaccessible, or barren place, a place devoid of anything good. Darkness reigns, light cannot penetrate, and evil abounds. A barren desert, perhaps, where nothing can grow, or the dark cell of the prisoner alone with his fears. A place identified by *the stark absence of God*. And on that cross, for the first time ever, Jesus felt—and was—separated from his Father, God. He was left alone in a place of absolute desolation.

C. S. Lewis described seeking God when he was happy as being "welcomed with open arms." But after the death of his beloved wife, when his need was desperate, he found a door slammed in his face, "and a sound of bolting and double bolting on the inside. After that, silence."[2]

C. S. Lewis was going through a spiritual experience that saints have long recognized and have coined as "the dark night of the soul." He felt separated from God, whose absence he experienced in profound feelings of loneliness and abandonment and in the experience of divine silence. Eventually, God reached into Lewis's pain, enabling him to identify his overwhelming feelings of grief with the sufferings and spiritual abandonment Jesus must have experienced.

Jesus is alone, pitched against all authorities. Everyone else seems to have their support systems, their networks. Yet, in this moment, Jesus is stripped of each, one after the other. He is against the Jewish religious authorities, he is standing alone against the Roman political authority, and even some of his own friends have disowned him. And now, separated from his Father, he has no blueprint to guide him—this is completely uncharted territory. He is *contra mundum*—against the world—and it is devastatingly painful. Terrifying. He seems to have reached true meaninglessness and total aloneness.

Yet even in this cry of desperation, there is intimacy and love: "My God, my God." In his moment of greatest suffering, it is Scripture that comes to the lips of Jesus. I have heard it said, "If you cut Scripture, it bleeds Jesus, and if you cut Jesus, he bleeds Scripture." And it is Psalm 22 that comes to his mind at the moment of his greatest trial, a psalm known to him from early childhood. Written by David hundreds of years before, it is an astonishing psalm to read.

Psalm 22

It is called a psalm of reorientation because the psalmist begins in a place of despair, but by the end his confidence in God is reaffirmed and hope is restored—the psalmist has been "reoriented." And, as we read it, we see that the Holy Spirit, the very Spirit of God that inspired David to write the psalm, was writing not only about David but about Jesus. It is remarkable how the psalm holds the tension between forsakenness and faithfulness.

"My God, my God, why have you forsaken me?" (v. 1).

"I've trusted you, and I am not disappointed" (v. 5 PAR).

It speaks so clearly of the cross: "I'm poured out, all my bones are out of joint, I can count them, I'm dried up" (v. 14 PAR).

"People stare and gloat over me. They divide my clothes among them and cast lots for my garment" (vv. 17–18).

And then David wrote, "He has not despised or scorned the suffering of the afflicted one" (v. 24). The word in Hebrew is close in meaning to "the only son"—"the afflicted only son."

"He's not despised the suffering of his only Son, all the families of the earth will remember him to the ends of the earth. Because he has done it" (vv. 27, 30–31 PAR).

The cross didn't take Jesus by surprise or catch God off guard. "Before the foundation of the world in the book of life . . . the Lamb . . . was slain" (Rev. 13:8 ESV). When God created the universe, he knew the cost of redeeming it. When he created human beings, he knew the cost of redeeming them. God loved his people so much that he was willing to pay the cost himself. The greatest agony he could ever experience unlocked the greatest opportunity Jesus would ever have to show his love for you.

The cross shows what the love of

When God created the universe, he knew the cost of redeeming it. When he created human beings, he knew the cost of redeeming them.

God looks like in a fallen world. God's love for his people will always surpass humanity's love for God. He counted the cost of knowing us and drawing us close, welcoming us home as much-loved sons and daughters before a day of our lives were lived, before we were ever born. To the extent that God loves, he chooses to suffer.

Gethsemane

In *His Dark Materials* trilogy of novels, author Philip Pullman imagines an even more radical experience of separation—a kind of severing of the self that might give us an insight into Jesus' experience. The world of the novels is a fantasy world similar but definitely not identical to our own world. Technologies, cities, cultures, and religions are recognizable yet subtly distorted to make the everyday strange. Similarly, the inhabitants of the world are recognizably human yet also very unlike you or me. Most strikingly, every person has a *daemon* in the form of an animal, which is a sort of manifestation of his or her own personality with which that person can share experiences and converse. It is an alter ego of some sort which, while not physically attached, must remain in very close proximity to its human counterpart.

In one of the most terrifying strands of a complex narrative, we learn that the forces of evil in the world, the Gobblers, have invented a machine that can harvest vast power by separating children from their daemons. The children survive the process but are shadows of their former selves, forever scarred by a fundamental loneliness and isolation that they could never have imagined or prepared for. Toward the end of the first book in the trilogy, one of these mutilated children is discovered clutching a piece of dried fish just as another was clutching her daemon against her heart. All he had was the dried fish—he had no daemon because the Gobblers had cut it away. The author describes a human being with no daemon "like someone without a face, or with their ribs laid open and their heart torn out."[3]

And so Jesus' ribs are laid bare and his heart torn in two as he is separated from the Father. But let us go back to the garden of Gethsemane on the night before the crucifixion. As we trace the story's development, from this point we can begin to understand the process that led to that separation, to the godforsakenness of God, if you will. You might remember what happened in the garden of Gethsemane.

Jesus was already suffering as he anticipated the fate that he knew awaited him. Anguished, he asked his closest disciples to stay and watch, to pray with and for him. Yet they fell asleep. So it was alone that Jesus prayed the prayer we know so well: "Abba, Father, everything is possible for you. Take this cup from me. Yet not what I will, but what you will" (Mark 14:36). At this point, in spite of the terrible suffering, we are told that blood was appearing on his forehead and falling to the ground like drops of sweat, and in spite of the knowledge that he would soon be going to the cross, still he can cry "Abba, Father."

Abba

In the garden, the unique intimacy of the Father, the Son, and the Holy Spirit is still intact. Jesus is physically lying down before the Father and simultaneously laying down all his fears and horrors. He is speaking to him in the closeness of the loving, tight-knit relationship they had enjoyed since before the dawn of time and that had been preserved even through Jesus' incarnation and life on earth. God being referred to as a warm, tenderhearted father is the radical unveiling of God through the revelation of Jesus.

The Gospel writers reveal to us that Jesus referred to God as "Abba" Father. It is a phrase Jesus used throughout his ministry, particularly as he related to God in prayer (Matt. 6:9–13). It was a term that would have been shocking in its usage to the Pharisees and religious leaders of the day. It was both radical and revolutionary to call God "Father," otherwise known as "Daddy." This encapsulates the nature of Jesus' relationship with the Father. It was so important to Jesus that when his disciples asked him to teach them to pray he gave them a model that began by uttering the word "Father" (Luke 11:2). Jesus called God the Father *Abba*, and he invites us to do the same. To fail to both recognize and adore God as Father in this way is to call into question whether we truly know the God we worship.

Even after Jesus leaves the garden, as he is tried and flogged and marched toward his death, still his relationship with his Father remains unbroken. Even on the hill of Golgotha, as great nails are driven through his wrists and feet, even as the cross is lifted and dropped into place, he can look down upon his tormenters and again speak to his Father. He says, "Father, forgive them, for they don't know what they are doing" (Luke 23:34). How unthinkably extraordinary is this outpouring of forgiveness. How, we wonder, in the very moment of his own torture and crucifixion, could he still think of others and pray that the closeness of the yet unbroken relationship with his Father might be experienced by those who were tormenting him?

But this beautiful intimacy is eventually shattered in the

cruelest way. Eventually, the desolation of separation from his Father overwhelms him and he cries out in anguish, naming an experience that was completely alien and—quite literally—unimaginable for him. *Forsaken.* It's amazing that he still has a voice at all at this stage in his suffering, considering the extraordinary pain he had gone through. But we read that it was in a "loud" voice that he cried out (the Greek word is *megas*, from which we get *megaphone*).

Can you even begin to imagine how weak he must have been on that cross, and yet in that loud voice he cries, "My God, my God, why have you forsaken me?" His cry is not understood. Those surrounding him mishear or misunderstand him. When he cries "My God, my God" (*Eloi, Eloi*), they seem to hear "Elijah, Elijah" (*Helias, Helias*) and believe he is calling upon the Old Testament prophet to come and rescue him.

There is confusion. The more compassionate of the onlookers offer him some cheap wine to quench his thirst and anesthetize the pain. But Jesus is not seeking rescue or comfort; he is suffering, but he knows this was always his destiny and his purpose. He does not drink wine for comfort but chooses instead to drink the cup of suffering down to the dregs in order to fulfill his mission.

Here we find ourselves at the center of the mystery, at the heart of the history of histories, at the very moment upon which the human story pivots. We might imagine the Father looking and seeing the Son upon the cross, and the Son realizing that the moment of death is upon him, that he is doing precisely what his Father wanted him to do, following the path he had chosen to its bitter end. In this moment, when the Son says, "My God, my God," we notice that for the first time he is not saying "Father," not "Abba, Daddy," but using another term, brutal in its detachment: "My

God." It is, of course, a statement of theological truth, but all the relational intimacy has been stripped away. It would be as if my son were to call me "parent" or Mr. Costa.

The loving closeness of the garden of Gethsemane, the loving prayerfulness even of the first moments upon the cross when he called for his Father to forgive his tormentors, have both disappeared. Jesus is still crying to "my" God, but the possessive pronoun only emphasizes and accentuates the pain. It would be understandable if he yelled *God!* as contemporary exclamations do. But "my" God, why are you—you who have loved me with absolute love, you who have never let me down or left me alone—why are you above all others, deserting me, abandoning me? *My* God, *my* God, why?

Why?

Why? That single word reverberates through every human population in every age, through every nation, tribe, and family that has ever existed, through the experience of every single person on the planet who has ever lived. At some point in our lives we will find ourselves asking, "Why?" Or, more likely, shouting, screaming, or crying, *"Why?"*

Why does a disease devastate whole populations? Why does a ferry go down with the men, women, and children on board lost? Why does an airplane disappear, leaving behind distraught relatives without even a shred of comfort from knowing what happened to their loved

> At some point in our lives we will find ourselves asking, "Why?" Or, more likely, shouting, screaming, or crying, *"Why?"*

ones? Why earthquakes? Why tsunamis? Why the subtle mutations in otherwise good cells that lead to cancer? Why is there sorrow, illness, violence, bereavement? Why are my prayers not answered?

Whenever we pray, cry, or scream, "Why?" we are, intentionally or otherwise, placing ourselves alongside Jesus in a kind of communion with the one who asked that same question of his Father. "Why? Why have you forsaken me, your very own Son?" We might feel so totally abandoned, so thoroughly rejected, so fundamentally lost that all we can do is cry, "Why?" Yet, in Jesus' cries from the depths of suffering and violence on the cross—the deepest grief ever known—he carried our *why* with him. We are not alone. He understands us, he's been there, and he assures us that he has a plan to wipe away every tear, to make "everything sad . . . come untrue," as J. R. R. Tolkien put it at the end of *The Lord of the Rings*. No one likes tough times, but those tests add power to our testimony.

If God didn't withhold from us his very own Son, will God withhold anything we need? Ann Voskamp put it eloquently: "If trust must be earned, hasn't God unequivocally earned our trust with the bark on the raw wounds, the thorns pressed into the brow, your name on the cracked lips? How will He not also graciously give us all things He deems best and right?"[4]

He's already given the incomprehensible. Timothy Keller wrote:

No matter what precautions we take, no matter how well we have put together a good life, no matter how hard we have worked to be healthy, wealthy, comfortable with friends and family, and successful with our career—something will inevitably ruin it. No amount of money, power, and planning can prevent bereavement, dire illness, relationship betrayal, financial disaster, or a host of other troubles from entering your life. Human life is fatally fragile and subject to forces beyond our power to manage. Life is tragic.[5]

Suffering is unbearable unless you know God is for you and God is with you. Because if we think amid our pain and suffering that we are forsaken, we could fall into three possible traps: isolation, self-absorption, and condemnation.

Isolation. Suffering can make you feel cut off from everyone else's everyday experiences, leaving you feeling isolated from your friends and family, whom you may feel can't really understand what it is you are going through. Many people may stay at a distance because a person who is suffering reminds them that none of us are truly in control of our lives. Suffering and turmoil can fall upon any of us.

> If God didn't withhold from us his very own Son, will God withhold anything we need?

Self-absorption. Suffering makes it hard for us to take our focus off of ourselves. Our pain absorbs every ounce of our head space, and it leaves no room for us to feel compassion or empathy for other people who are suffering.

Condemnation. When unexpected, excruciating suffering arrives at our door, it is hard to avoid feeling as though we are being judged or punished for some behavior or some action that we have previously taken.

But back to our story. We have noted that when Jesus cried out, it was with a *loud* voice. That adjective reminds us of another incident right at the start of Jesus' ministry—another loud voice. In the moment of his baptism by John in the Jordan River, we are told that there was a loud voice from heaven, which proclaimed, "This is my beloved Son." At the same moment, a dove was seen to descend from heaven to alight upon Jesus. This was the confirmation by the Holy Spirit of the words that were spoken from heaven. The Holy Spirit confirmed the love of the Father for his Son, Jesus. And so we would do well never to forget that the same Holy Spirit who affirmed the Father and Son's loving relationship at the start was also present alongside Jesus in the garden of Gethsemane and on the cross itself, even at the moment of abandonment.

We must not think for a second that the Father was sitting safe and untroubled in heaven, detached and unconcerned as he watched his Son suffering. This was not the case at all. This was a moment of suffering and crisis for the Father as much as for the Son. He experienced the desolation of the loss of his Son, just as the Son experienced the anguish of the loss of his Father. Jesus found himself fatherless, disowned, and disinherited. The experience of the Father cannot really be named; it remains in the realms of deep mystery. Clearly, there was loss and deprivation, but it's unfathomable. But it is the consistent, faithful presence of the Holy Spirit that provides the glimmer of hope in the midst of the despair. The Spirit holds the Father and Son together in love even as their intimacy is threatened to the breaking point by the cross.

The Holy Spirit is the life-giving Spirit, and he led Jesus through a life of ministry and healing and power to the place of sacrifice and suffering, to death and loss. These were places Jesus had to pass through as he was led into life through the resurrection. Here is the extraordinary truth: love was still flowing in deep and hidden channels even at this time of suffering, judgment, and separation.

And so I find I have the audacity to claim that there are glorious implications for us, and the way we live, in the story of Jesus being forsaken, however paradoxical that sentence might seem. I would like to mention three.

First, we can choose a Spirit-led walk. When we look to the cross, we see that this God alone is for us because this God alone has been one of us. How else could he have been our Savior if he hadn't known suffering himself? How could we relate to him and how could we understand us if he wasn't wounded? We can know that there is no situation or trouble that we will ever go through where Jesus isn't standing with us and cannot understand.

Perhaps you come to this book wondering why God seems to have abandoned you. Maybe you feel battered and bruised, broken down by the turbulent storms and trials of life. Remember that our times of loss or abandonment or uncertainty are marked by the presence of the Spirit, just as Jesus' moment of forsakenness was marked by the presence of the Spirit.

> We can know that there is no situation or trouble that we will ever go through where Jesus isn't standing with us and cannot understand.

That is why it is so significant that the curtain was torn in two. It used to be, in the old days of the temple, that if you were a woman, child, or foreigner, you had no hope of entering the Holy Place. If you were a man, you might have the chance of being a priest, but even if you were a priest, you could never enter the Most Holy Place unless you were a chief priest. And even if you were chief priest you could only enter the Most Holy Place once a year in fear and in trembling. Such was the fear of the holiness of God. But a curtain forty feet high and as thick as a wall is rent down the center, ripped from top to bottom, removing the divide between God and humanity as redemption flows out to all humankind. So all people can approach and know intimacy with God. Every human being that professes faith in Jesus can come into his presence.

Maybe, amid the struggles that you face, you might want to ask him to give you a greater glimpse of the cost so you might feel the extent and the greatness of his love for you. You're secure in his grip because he loves you, and nothing can separate you from his love. If you doubt that in any way, look at the cross and see his great love for you. See him forsaken so that you don't have to be, although, of course, we are not promised a life free from abandonment. People will abandon us, just as the disciples abandoned Jesus in the garden of Gethsemane. Occasionally the pain of our circumstances can cause us to look around, wondering if God has abandoned us as well. But we can expect to be led by the Holy Spirit through the valleys of life, not just to the mountaintops.

Second, we can adopt a Spirit-led worldview. From the ruins we can rejoice because God still reigns. The mercies of God will never let us down, and his mercy insulates the outer circumference of our lives amid the troubles, challenges, and difficulties of our lives.

> **The Spirit comforts us and cries: "There *is* possibility, there *is* hope, there *is* God even in the worst moments of your life!"**

The masculine noun in Hebrew for *mercy* is the word *rechem*. The root of the word refers to the deep love found or rooted in some natural bond such as childbirth. It describes a deep inner feeling we can know as compassion, and this compassion is what epitomizes God's mercy—a mercy that insulates our inadequacies and sufferings, a mercy that insulates the abused and hopeless. In the midst of such pain, the Spirit comforts us and cries: "There *is* possibility, there *is* hope, there *is* God even in the worst moments of your life!"

Third, when we look at Christ being forsaken on the cross, *it enables us to fight a Spirit-led war.* It's at the cross that sin met its match. The veil in the temple was rent in two, so there is no longer a divide between the common and the hallowed, and the whole earth is full of God's glory. Christ is no longer nailed to the cross; he is seated at the right hand of the Father in power and glory, with everything as his footstool. The only thing nailed to the cross is our sin.

And so it is that the enemy has ultimately been defeated, and we can withstand the fiery trials that are sent our way. We don't work to come into Christ's presence; when we place our trust in him, his presence enters us. He didn't come just to reveal the nature of his strange kingdom; he came to reconcile us to himself and to live within us. We have the opportunity to join the multitudes who have gone before us, and the masses who will come after, who at times got defeated, soiled by life, and beset by trials, wearing the bloodied garments of life's tribulations, but through it all clinging to the cross of Christ.

It is a strange kingdom indeed when suffering and abandonment are transformed into the power of God's presence and love. The sorrow that hurts you? God can fashion it into faith that sustains you. The grief that shattered your heart? God crafts that into unshakable faith. The loss you never expected? God molds that into strength you can't explain. He loves the disconnected, the discarded, the disenfranchised. Those who are categorically or specifically "dissed." Even death won't hold fear for us, as Christ has claimed us. No present predicament or future contingency can change his unconditional love for us. So you can know your future is secure and you are held firmly by Jesus, and once he grabs hold he never lets go.

You can know your future is secure and you are held firmly by Jesus, and once he grabs hold he never lets go.

Jesus makes our low places stepping stones to climb higher with him if we take our thorns of grief to the throne of grace because there sits our godforsaken Messiah, who knew no one higher and yet lowered himself to the lowest point. For you, for me, for all. Our grief doesn't need to be suppressed, we don't grieve alone, and there is hope beyond the grave. Death doesn't have the last word. Jesus has defeated it. And one day he will remove it entirely. On that day God will wipe away all our tears and bury our grief for good.

And so it is that we embrace the mystery, the paradox at the heart of the cross: that in Christ's experience of being God-forsaken, we know we need never face suffering alone. If you are going through a period of darkness and it feels as if God has abandoned you, don't let it drive you to despair. Instead, if Jesus went through it, why not you? If C. S. Lewis went through it, why not you?

God is with you through divorce, he is with you through failure, he is with you through bereavement, through disappointment, through fear and guilt and shame. He is with you through the deepest despair and the most savage betrayal. Let me encourage you with the promises of Scripture: if God is letting you go through the valley and you are in a time of great testing where you feel separated from him, you can be absolutely certain that even this separation cannot ultimately frustrate God's grand scheme and story.

Jesus promised: "Never will I leave you, nor forsake you" (Heb. 13:5 PAR). Therefore, one thing is without doubt. If you are feeling isolated, alone, and abandoned, there will come a time when God will reveal himself to you again. And when that happens, you will come out more mature in your faith and with a much stronger sense of who God is and how much he cares about you. You may perceive that God is absent, but "neither death nor life, neither angels nor demons, neither the present nor the future, nor any powers, neither height nor depth,

> **God is with you through divorce, he is with you through failure, he is with you through bereavement, through disappointment, through fear and guilt and shame.**

nor anything else in all creation, will be able to separate us from the love of God that is in Christ Jesus our Lord" (Rom. 8:38–39).

The forsakenness of Christ is a promise of God's eternal presence.

A Time to Meditate

Music

- "Clinging to the Cross," Tim Hughes
- *Adagietto, Symphony 5*, Mahler

Reflect

- "My God, my God, why have you forsaken me?" We hear the torment in his cry. Jesus is, for the first time, separated from God. But still he says, *"My* God." All of us know times of darkness, though for some of us it's darker than for others. Abandonment, loneliness, fear, grief, rejection, and pain. And in response at times, only divine silence. Just like Jesus. Perhaps all we can manage, with him, is *"My* God, *my* God, *my* God."

- But the same Holy Spirit who affirmed the loving relationship between Father and Son in the waters of the Jordan River is present in the garden of Gethsemane and even at that moment of agony and abandonment on the cross. However dark things are, we can still say, "Come, Holy Spirit!"

- The curtain was ripped in two. There is now no barrier between us and God. All of us can come into his presence. That's you. And me. And now. And always. All we need to do is take a step forward. The forsakenness of Christ has become a promise of God's eternal presence. He is with us.

Prayer

Lord, we know that you have suffered for us, you have suffered like us, and you suffer with us. And we know that your time of abandonment was our promise of your presence. And, as we thank you, we pray for an increasing awareness of you with us, amen.

THREE

FINISHED

Later, knowing that everything had now been finished, and so that Scripture would be fulfilled, Jesus said, "I am thirsty." A jar of wine vinegar was there, so they soaked a sponge in it, put the sponge on a stalk of the hyssop plant, and lifted it to Jesus' lips. When he had received the drink, Jesus said, "It is finished." With that, he bowed his head and gave up his spirit.

—John 19:28–30

I WANT TO BEGIN THIS CHAPTER BY TELLING YOU THE true story of a terrible tragedy that happened thirty years ago. Just sixty seconds out of the Belgian port of Zeebrugge, a ferry carrying more than 500 passengers took on water and capsized, killing 193 people. The disaster shocked the whole nation and went down as one of the worst catastrophes in maritime history. The bow doors had been left open, water flooded in, and the whole vessel went down astonishingly quickly.

It was a horrific disaster, and yet within it, there was an act of extraordinary heroism. The reason I am particularly drawn to this story is that one of the heroes was a colleague of mine at the time in the city of London. This young man saw that great cataracts of water were pouring into one of the windows as the ferry listed heavily to one side. And beyond, trapped, he saw a woman and her child. They were stuck on the wrong side of the chasm created by the inrushing water, away from the doorway and the stairs up to the deck and salvation.

On the one side of the raging water was safety and on the other side was certain drowning and death. My colleague, Andrew Parker, lay himself down across the torrent of water, and the woman and the child literally clambered over his body to safety. As others emerged, also on the wrong side of the torrent of water, he remained there to provide the pathway to life for many. The newspapers dubbed him the "human bridge."

The Weight and Problem of Sin

What is it that threatens to sweep us away from safety, from groundedness, from life in all its fullness? We must not downplay or neglect the weight and problem of our sin, a word we hear little of today, a word we often try to dilute or soften or gloss over. We would rather call our wrongdoing a silly mistake or a foolish choice. But while mistakes and foolishness are definitely part of the human experience, sin is rebellion against God.

Sin results in a breach of our relationship with God, places us on the wrong side of the torrent, and subjects us to judgment and death. Perhaps the defining characteristic of sin in our time is seen in our desire to "go it alone." It is no coincidence that Frank Sinatra's "I Did It My Way" is a song frequently played at funerals.

From the Bible to popular culture, we can just glance at the most popular characters in recent fiction to see another indication of our misguided passion for independence. Think of James Bond, Jack Reacher, Jason Bourne, and Katniss Everdeen of the Hunger Games franchise, and after that an endless stream of superheroes. All of them are defined by an incredible degree of self-sufficiency. They are heroes because they need nothing and no one. They can do it all and they can do it all on their own! Foolishly, we continue to celebrate this myth of the self-made man or woman, downplaying the contribution of those—parents, teachers, friends, colleagues—who made the success possible and willfully ignoring the One who gave us life in the first place.

This warped desire for independence, self-sufficiency, and unshared credit for our own achievements lies right at the root of sin. In the opening chapters of the Bible in the book of Genesis, we see that the man and woman, living in paradise and lacking nothing, were still discontent. They ate of the tree because they sought to become like God themselves, sought to take total control of their own lives through knowledge of good and evil, sought to stop being creatures and become the Creator. We blindly imitate their self-destructive pursuit of independence, choosing to go our own way even when in our heart of hearts we know we are all at sea, unable to plot a safe course toward or even to correctly identify the things that will make us truly and securely happy.

The prophet Isaiah drew on some pastoral imagery to highlight our misguided attempts at independence: "All we like sheep have gone astray; we have turned—every one—to his own way; and the LORD has laid on him the iniquity of us all" (Isa. 53:6 ESV).

In choosing to do his Father's will rather than his own, in choosing to remember his dependence rather than pursue the illusion of independence, Jesus somehow undid the actions of Adam and Eve in the garden and released humanity from the dreadful consequences of their sin. He took the shame of our foolhardy struggle for independence upon himself and suffered the resulting separation from God—the godforsakenness we spoke of in the last chapter. His obedience washed away the stain of our disobedience. A life focused on self-fulfillment is really to our self-detriment. The most miserable place to be trapped is inside yourself.

Jesus lay himself down and made a bridge for us from selfishness and death to love and life. We have a choice whether to cross that bridge or not. That woman and her child on the ferry at Zeebrugge had a choice to make. They could have remained where they were and been swept away by the torrents of water to a cruel and certain death. But they saw the bridge that led to safety and survival,

> **The most miserable place to be trapped is inside yourself.**

and, without hesitating, they stumbled headlong across my friend Andrew's body. They chose life. And we can as well.

Tetelestai

The words *it is finished* are translated from the Greek word *tetelestai*, the word an artist might use when applying the final brush stroke to a masterpiece, or the word a builder might say when placing the final brick. It is also a word that was often written on parchment to acknowledge receipt of payment in the early first and second centuries. It acted like the modern-day receipt Apple sends via e-mail after a customer purchases a new product. The receipt confirms to both the customer and the company that payment has been made in full. Jesus' death on the cross was the complete and final payment for sin—it is accomplished; the work is done. This is not a declaration of defeat, but a cry of completion. God has finished what only God could finish.

But what exactly is finished? What did Jesus mean in that morbid God-forsaken moment, at the apex of excruciating pain, on the edge of death? Physically, his fight was over. Jesus, who was fully human, had endured too much, and physiologically, his life was finished. There was no more breath left in his lungs, his heart had been stretched too far, and he had no more to give. The life of Jesus Christ of Nazareth was finished. But the words resound more deeply than a biological statement of fact. It wasn't just a physical endurance battle that he had been fighting. Jesus had taken on the sins of all humanity, he had absorbed all the evil forces at work in our world, and he had completed the battle. He had "disarmed the powers and authorities, [and] made a public spectacle of them, triumphing over them by the cross" (Col. 2:15).

The powers and authorities? Evil? Sin? The concepts are strange. And how could Paul have used the word *triumphing* in the context of a bloody man, near naked and exposed, stripped of everything, to describe this moment? It looked like a defeat of the cruelest kind. Yet it was the very power that frees us from our sin and transgressions. Jesus pleaded our case on behalf of us and took our punishment, paying the ultimate price, so that when we stand accused by others for our sins and shortcomings, we have an advocate who overrules our accusers.

In 1850 Nathaniel Hawthorne published a novel called *The Scarlet Letter*. In this book a woman named Hester is caught cheating on her husband and found guilty of infidelity. The authorities demand that she wear a letter *A* on her dress as the symbol of her adultery and shame. As I reflected on this, I thought to myself that we often do the same thing. We are quick to label people by the mistakes they've made or by one aspect of their character. Whether it's an *I* for infidelity, a *G* for greed, or an *S* for selfishness, that isn't how God sees us or identifies us. He takes off our grave clothes of sin and shame and renames us as chosen, loved, and held in the beloved. He gives us a new identity and hope for the future.

There is a story in John's Gospel that is similar to *The Scarlet Letter*. Like Hester, a woman is caught having an affair, and the Pharisees of the day are ready to stone her to death when Jesus steps in. Jesus doesn't defend her adulterous behavior, but he does defend her—in the spirit of an advocate, not an accuser. And his defense is like that of a seasoned lawyer. In a sentence, he finishes the argument: "Let any one of you who is without sin be the first to throw a stone at her" (John 8:7). Each religious leader at the scene moves forward, and they all drop the stones clenched in their hands and turn to walk away. Then Jesus turns to the woman caught in adultery and says, "Go now and leave your life of sin" (v. 11).

Whereas the Pharisees were writing this woman off, Jesus was writing her into his story. Jesus totally changes the woman's circumstances, and no doubt her future, and turns her toward him. This is the moment this woman can receive a new identity and a new hope for the future. It turns her greatest mistake into a wonderful story of redemption: "Go now and leave your life of sin."

Paul could call the cross a triumph because it is something utterly complete—there is nothing that we can add to it. We will never run out of grace or mercy; we will always be able to withdraw from the account that was settled by Christ on our behalf.

This is why the image that Paul used in his letter to the Colossians is taken from the triumphal military processions that followed after a victory. Frequently, the official representative of the vanquished army, perhaps a general, would be stripped of his robes and all the other manifestations of his authority. He would be humiliated, disarmed, deprived of every vestige of power and authority. He would be a captive of war. But on the cross, the one who appeared vanquished and humiliated, suffering the cruelest of deaths, was actually the one who would emerge victorious, humiliating the very powers and principalities that sought to subdue him in the first place.

We will never run out of grace or mercy; we will always be able to withdraw from the account that was settled by Christ on our behalf.

"It is finished." On a macro level, the powers and principalities of a broken world where evil flourishes are finished. And on a micro level, the sin all human beings have carried in their hearts since that moment in the garden of Eden is finished. And yet we evidently live in a world where evil, on a universal and a local level, seems far from finished. In fact, it appears to be flourishing. Professor Christina Hoff Sommers, a notable philosopher and ethicist, said, "We have been thrown back into a moral Stone Age."[1] We may have achieved huge technological advances but there is an almost retrograde step in our humanity and morality.

Did Jesus really mean what he said? How do we reconcile the apparent triumph on the cross with the realities of today? The evil regimes, the systemic injustices, war and the threat of war, the senseless massacre of the innocent, to name but a few. Our disordered world shows how quickly we take our focus off God. Sin takes root in our hearts: visible in our greed, in our promiscuity, in our desire for preferment, in our desperation to achieve even at the expense of others, in our inhuman coldness toward the plight of others. We cannot escape from the reality of sin and its consequences all around us.

We recognize that a battle rages in every place where human beings are gathered—in nations and institutions—and also in the heart of each one of us. At times the battle appears only to be magnifying, with the forces of evil in full flood. But it is in the very midst of the battle that we are called to exercise the belief that the words *it is finished* do apply even to the most pernicious evils that abound. Jesus Christ did overcome all these powers and it is our choice, our decision, to claim that triumph of Jesus and make it manifest in our lives today.

When Jesus said, "It is finished," he did not mean, "I am finished." After all, we know that three days later he rose from the dead. When he said, "It is finished," he meant that the work he had been asked to do by the Father was complete. Jesus had followed his road, the path of obedience and sacrifice, to its bitter end. By becoming one of us and dying on the cross and rising from the dead three days later, he built a bridge between death and life, between bondage to sin and freedom.

The film *Saving Private Ryan* is set in the Second World War, and it tells the story of a group of soldiers who are given orders to rescue one soldier from behind enemy lines in Normandy, France. This particular soldier had three brothers, and all of them had recently been killed, leaving him as the only child of a single mother. When the United States' chief of staff hears about her situation, he gives orders that the precious remaining son, Private James Ryan, must be protected at all costs. He sends a team of soldiers to bring him back alive. But it's a dangerous mission; he is behind enemy lines, and, one by one, the soldiers die. At one stage of the mission, the captain says, "He better be worth it. He better go home and cure a disease or invent a longer-lasting lightbulb."

In the final scene, set on a heavily shelled bridge as the captain himself dies, he looks into the eyes of Private Ryan and whispers, "James, earn this . . . earn it." Fifty years pass, and, in the closing shots of the film, an elderly James Ryan kneels beside the captain's grave and says, "Every day I think about what you said to me that day on the bridge. I've tried to live my life the best that I could. I hope that was enough. I hope that, at least in your eyes, I've earned what all you have done for me." And then, weeping, he turns to his wife and says: "Tell me I have led a good life. . . . Tell me I'm a good man."

In one sense, those final words of the captain—"earn it"— have slowly crushed Private Ryan. The burden of trying to earn the sacrifice made by the captain has affected the whole of his life.

But Jesus' last words are very different. As Jesus died to rescue us, he didn't say, "Fight to earn this." Rather, he said, "It is finished." Those three words are so simple, and yet the impact of them is of cosmic significance. Those three words have the power to affect the whole of our lives and every living soul on the planet.

God Bridged the Gap

"It is finished." Those three words give us the assurance that the bridge between humankind and God is intact. There is a safe passage to cross over. In a world that has become disconnected, where we would rather text than talk, where we would rather tweet than meet, God bridged the gap between broken humanity and perfect divinity to bring true connection and true intimacy to reconcile our fragmented relationships. We so desperately need this bridge because of what sin can do. I want to highlight three things that might help us acknowledge the need we all have for God.

Sin creates distance. When Adam and Eve were first in the garden, there was no distance between them and God. They walked in perfect unity with each other and with the Lord. But when sin entered the picture, the first thing God said was, "Adam, where are you?" That was not to say that God did not know where Adam was; it was more indicative of a wedge that had come between them. They were no longer operating in harmony with one another. Distance existed, which didn't exist before sin entered Eden.

> "It is finished." Those three words give us the assurance that the bridge between humankind and God is intact.

Sin cultivates shame. I've done things to displease God, and I've experienced the overwhelming sense of shame that kicks in when I know that I have hurt God. Shame tarnishes the relationship between humans and God because shame makes us wish there was no God. Shame has the power to make people feel that their inadequacies are exposed and that they cannot bear for other people—or worst of all, God—to see who they really are because they might be rejected. And so there is a deep unease within people's hearts.

But that is the deep mystery of the cross: Jesus was captured and shamed so that humanity might be free from shame; he died in darkness so that all people might be able to live in the light. He took not only the guilt but also the shame away, building a bridge for humanity to step over and be free. Sin, guilt, and condemnation want to hold people hostage, but the power of the blood is no longer "shame on you" but shame *off* you.

Sin corrupts intimacy. In the garden, Adam said, "I was naked; so I hid" (Gen. 3:10). Adam and Eve were naked and unashamed, but when sin came in, they were ashamed of their nakedness. Where previously they had enjoyed full intimacy, now they tried to cover up. If there is any unconfessed sin in our lives, we have a choice to try to cover it up, which is ultimately impossible, or to come and uncover it at the foot of the cross. The blood of Jesus is the bridge to cross over into freedom and newness of life.

Jesus, the bridge between our humanity and divinity, lived a sinless, spotless life for thirty-three years, building bridges not just spiritually but relationally. Jesus had conversations with nonbelievers all the time, and he engaged in conversation with those

> **The blood of Jesus is the bridge to cross over into freedom and newness of life.**

eschewed by the Jewish rabbis. Jesus stretched himself and became the bridge over which other people might experience the grace of God.

We all have the choice. And it's only when we say yes that we can stretch beyond what we thought was possible in our own strength and discover his strength that we never knew we had. Our comfort zones can so easily turn into death traps of complacency when we stay on one side of the chasm. Our transgressions, the bad things that we have done and the good things we have left undone, always threaten to drag us under and separate us from our Father.

The shame we feel, the selfish anger we direct at those around us, the greed we can't get rid of, the unwholesome habits that have come to typify our daily life, they wrap their cold tendrils around our ankles and suck us downward. On the other side of the bridge is the place of safety and security and fullness of life, where we can live free from the hurts and mistakes of the past.

Jesus' words on the cross—"It is finished"—sound as if they speak of an end, but could they actually signal a new beginning?

A Strange Cry of Victory

"It is finished!" is a cry of victory. A rather strange cry, but a triumphant cry nonetheless. What Christ came to do has been done once and for all. But now we live amid the tension of knowing Christ has won the day, but waking up knowing things aren't yet how they should be—knowing that we are to live in the present, looking for signs of this completed work.

It could be in the office, in the meeting, or during the busy morning commute, but we must remind ourselves each day that the cross is not a defeat but the victory of God the Father. Jesus' death was not in vain. On the contrary, Jesus is seated at the right hand of the Father in the heavenly places (Eph. 1:20). Not only is he seated at the right hand of the Father, but he is interceding for us (Rom. 8:34).

Paul wrote to the Colossians:

> Now I rejoice in what I am suffering for you, and I fill up in my flesh what is still lacking in regard to Christ's afflictions, for the sake of his body, which is the church. I have become its servant by the commission God gave me to present to you the word of God in its fullness—the mystery that has been kept hidden for ages and generations, but is now disclosed to the Lord's people. To them God has chosen to make known among the Gentiles the glorious riches of this mystery, which is Christ in you, the hope of glory. (1:24–27)

The apostle John, the only apostle who stood at the foot of the cross when Jesus died, later in his life received a vision of the climax to human history. He saw the new heaven and the new earth, and he saw a new Jerusalem descend from heaven. He saw Jesus sit on the throne, and we hear Jesus say, "It is done! It is finished!" (Rev. 21).

God has finished what God began. Jesus' atoning sacrifice on the cross is of eternal importance and significance. It means his ultimate sacrifice, lying on the altar on our behalf, makes it possible to live in a way that pleases him, glorifies his name, and witnesses to others. "It is finished" means Jesus has the victory, but the battle is not yet over. The war is still raging, and we must fight.

Human beings were created for relationship with God—Father, Son, and Holy Spirit. True human flourishing is only possible there, on the other side of the bridge, in the light and warmth of that divine relationship. Jesus Christ is the bridge between the place of judgment and death and the place of life. "Although we cannot alter the past, we can put our past upon the 'altar' as an act of worship."[2] He can redeem it and renew it, rebuilding and restoring us in the process and rewriting both my story and yours. Christianity was never meant to be an invoice to be paid, but an inheritance we are invited to receive.

You may have come to a point in your life when you feel that *it is finished*, or even that *you are finished*. But if you feel that, you are wrong. The end of a relationship, the end of a job or a career, the end of a phase or a stage or a season of your life— none of these is the end of you. That part of your life may be finished. But it doesn't mean that you are finished. The end of one phase of your life is not the end of your destiny. The end of a dream could be the precursor to a new dawn. Coming to the end of one path might bring you to the beginning of a fresh road and a whole new journey.

> He can redeem [the past] and renew it, rebuilding and restoring us in the process and rewriting both my story and yours.

Through the power of the Spirit released into the world through his death and resurrection, the rough edges of our disobedience can be transformed. Jesus' obedience came with a steep price tag, but the warranty is invaluable. If we trust in him, the rubble that is left by our failed attempt to run our own lives can be rebuilt into a new kind of life infused by the power of the Spirit.

Sir Winston Churchill is often listed among the greatest prime ministers in British history. He was certainly prodigiously talented. In addition to the many political offices he held across his long career, he won the Nobel Prize for literature, his paintings were critically acclaimed, and he also found time for journalism and frontline soldiering. There were times, however, when few would have thought him likely to leave such a great legacy.

His performance in the First World War had been mixed at best. As first lord of the Admiralty, he was held responsible for the disaster at Gallipoli, one of the most terrible debacles of the conflict. Later, as chancellor of the Exchequer in peacetime, he made the controversial decision to return Britain to the gold standard—a decision that was considered partly responsible for the painful deflation in the economy. By the 1930s such baggage, along with taking unpopular positions on a number of issues, led to his being cast out into the political wilderness.

Churchill could have been forgiven for thinking his best years were behind him, that he was finished. Yet we now know that his greatest successes were still ahead of him. In 1940, following the resignation of Neville Chamberlain, he became prime minister. Through the darkest days of the early years of the war, when Britain stood practically alone against Nazi aggression, he was the inspirational and bulldog-stubborn leader that history eulogizes.

Of course, these stories of fresh starts after apparent dead ends are not all played out on the world stage. The vast majority of new beginnings following disappointment and failure are more personal and domestic. The Australian broadcaster, Sheridan Voysey, wrote in *Resurrection Year* about the way in which he and his wife came to terms with the fact that they would not be able to have children. The book shows that, after the death of that dream, they were able to move on with their lives and begin a new adventure on the other side of the world, in Oxford. In his author's note, Sheridan observes that most of us have dreams, "precious gifts of the imagination," that give purpose and shape to our lives. As we grow older, however, we see many dreams die, including those closest to our hearts, like Sheridan's dream of a family. Yet he wrote his book in the belief that "perhaps a greater tragedy than a broken dream is a life forever defined by it."[3] There is always hope, even after we have said or felt that it is finished.

To me, this is such a relief. As I think about all the competing demands for my time and attention, all my mixed motivations, my dreams and desires, if I heard Jesus say to me, "Make yourself worthy of my sacrifice; earn it," that would slowly crush me. I would struggle under the weight of it. But if I wake up and spend time in his presence daily and hear him say on the cross, "It is finished," then that frees me from trying to earn his approval, trying to earn his love, and instead I can respond with thankfulness, because his love is the greatest motivator I can ever imagine.

> **There is always hope, even after we have said or felt that it is finished.**

I encourage you to look at the cross and to allow gratitude to well up in your heart: thankfulness that the greatest battle humankind could ever have to fight has already been fought; thankfulness that the greatest test anyone could ever have to face has been endured on humanity's behalf; thankfulness that the greatest obstacle has been removed, that the greatest opponent is defeated, that the greatest challenge is conquered.

Because God loves us, he doesn't say, "Now go and earn it." He says, "I love you this much." When we truly embrace this truth, we find there is rest in our hearts. We rest not on our own efforts but on the foundation and assurance of what Jesus has done for us. In a time of monumental challenge, God drew alongside Moses and said, "My Presence will go with you, and I will give you rest" (Ex. 33:14). And he says this to us again today.

Let us remember these truths when it looks as if the world is descending into a new dark age of inhumanity, cruelty, and oppression. We must remind ourselves that the cross has already determined the fate of these forces of evil. We may not see it immediately, but ultimately good will triumph. Piece by piece, in myriad individual struggles against difficult circumstances, the right side wins. The final triumph may arrive on the back of the countless small battles fought day-to-day by those who trust in the blood of Jesus Christ, as they work to see Christ's kingdom come in their own lives and in the lives of people they meet.

Let us live our lives in the knowledge that the victory has already been achieved. Let the words *it is finished* fill our minds and hearts as we face our battles, and hold tight, for whether in this life or in the next, the dawn of the Resurrection Day will come.

Trust him. Be hopeful. He is the bridge to living life in all its fullness.

A Time to Meditate

Music

- "It Is Finished," Matt Redman
- "Crucifixus" from Nicene Creed, Antonio Lotti

Reflect

- "It is finished!" says Jesus. He doesn't say, "Earn it!" It would crush us. He says it's complete. It's done. It's not about you being good. It's about God being good. His love will always surpass our love. We are reassured beyond doubt and for all time. Spend a moment thanking God for the power of "It is finished."

- Take a moment now to look up at the cross, and allow gratitude to well up in your heart. "I love you this much," says God to you, "and I made a bridge." The bridge is the cross, and you're invited to cross over. From bondage to freedom. From the old life to the new life. You can leave behind all that you wish you hadn't done or been or said. So, in his presence, you can say sorry and you can say thank you, and then you can name what you'd like to leave behind. And then you just need to leave it behind. And that's it!

- It's finished. It's done. It's time to go from partly living to fully living. In him. With him. For him. Hold tight. Trust God. Be hopeful. Are you ready to go?

Prayer

Lord, thank you that we don't have to earn it. Thank you that what you did is complete. Thank you for offering us through the cross a bridge to a new life—life in all its fullness. I'm ready for it. Thank you for always being ready for me, amen.

FOUR

FORGIVEN

Jesus said, "Father, forgive them, for they do not know what they are doing." And they divided up his clothes by casting lots. The people stood watching, and the rulers even sneered at him. They said, "He saved others; let him save himself if he is God's Messiah, the Chosen One." The soldiers also came up and mocked him. They offered him wine vinegar and said, "If you are the king of the Jews, save yourself." There was a written notice above him, which read: THIS IS THE KING OF THE JEWS. One of the criminals who hung there hurled insults at him: "Aren't you the Messiah? Save yourself and us!" But the other criminal rebuked him. "Don't you fear God," he said, "since you are under the same sentence? We are punished justly, for we are getting what our deeds deserve. But this man has done nothing wrong." Then he said, "Jesus, remember me when you come into your kingdom." Jesus answered him, "Truly I tell you, today you will be with me in paradise."

—Luke 23:34–43

JESUS HAD BEEN BETRAYED BY ONE OF HIS OWN

disciples for thirty pieces of silver. He had been arrested, interrogated, and tried with falsified evidence by the Jewish ruling council of his day. Peter, who was his most vocal supporter, had denied him, and Pontius Pilate and Herod Antipas had questioned his motives and authenticity. He had been whipped profusely, mocked with profanity, and paraded around as a laughingstock: a fake king with a crown of thorns on his head. Not only that, but he had been forced to carry the very instrument of his own execution on his back. If we imagine ourselves in Jesus' position, looking down at the crowd whose schemes and strategies had put us there, what would our first words be? Would they be words of mercy and grace?

The words that fell from Jesus' parched lips were: "Father, forgive them." Instead of asking God to give his killers their just deserts, Jesus asked him to bestow complete forgiveness on them. Jesus was neither condoning their actions nor denying their guilt, but rather recognizing that they didn't understand the weight of what they were doing. From the Jewish perspective, Jesus was a blasphemer against the God of the Torah; the Romans thought they were punishing another rabble-rousing criminal. They didn't realize they were committing the worst crime in the history of the world: the crucifiction of the Son of God.

Jesus interceded on behalf of the people who were torturing him, and at Golgotha he modeled the words he had shared again and again in his earthly ministry: "Love your enemies and pray for those who persecute you" (Matt. 5:44). And that's what he is still doing more than two thousand years later. From the throne room of heaven, Jesus is not accusing us but is standing as our advocate and interceding on our behalf.

Jesus is the Lamb who was slain—our Great High Priest who could atone for our sin, once and for all. That's why the writer of Hebrews said, "There have been many of those priests, since death prevented them from continuing in office" (7:23). But because Jesus lives for eternity, he has a permanent priesthood and lives to intercede for his children. When I think of where I fall short on a daily basis, it is a huge comfort to remember that Jesus is interceding for me and has the power to forgive me. When Jesus said, "Father, forgive them," his blood was already falling from his battered and bruised body, flowing from the cross toward us, and it is still flowing today. It covers every sin, every stain, and every act of shame, and it cleanses us from all unrighteousness (1 John 1:9).

But let us examine further this extraordinary forgiveness offered by Jesus on the cross. I have always thought that forgiveness presented God with a challenging problem, if I might put it that way. How can God show both his endless love for human beings who have broken their relationship with him and, at the same time, his utter rejection of humanity's sin? As we have seen, our separation from God is addressed by the death of Jesus upon the cross. As we saw in the last chapter, the cross is a bridge, and, as we choose to pass over it, we are reconciled to and reunited with our God. Though we are reconciled, this grace isn't free from any cost—it cost God everything. But, from our side, this grace is free, in that we need pay nothing; we need only cross the bridge through repentance.

And so to the meaning of repentance. "Forgive and forget" is a popular phrase and trips alliteratively off the tongue. We sin, we are forgiven, job done. We all love shortcuts. Even as I've typed this manuscript, "control Z" has been my best friend, undoing my last action so easily and effectively. Our separation from God, however, is not so easy. There is a little more to it, given the sacrifice and suffering that Jesus went through to enable forgiveness in the first place. True heartfelt repentance acknowledges the cost of the cross and is a visceral and necessary step on the way to truest freedom.

To deny the cost of the cross would be what Bonhoeffer termed "cheap grace": forgiveness without repentance, but with mere regret or remorse.

We need to go through a process for the transaction to be truly meaningful. The availability of God's forgiveness is no excuse for us to keep sinning. If anything, it is our greatest motivation to change.

I remember one of the apartheid survivors from South Africa, who had spent long periods in prison, telling me that we should try to *forgive* those who had shown such profound and damaging racial prejudice to so many for so long. That was difficult enough, but, he said, we must never *forget*—in order to ensure that the wrongs of the past remain fresh and are not repeated by another generation.

Often we want to ignore, deny, or conceal a wrong and act as if it never happened. But the damage done to human hearts by sin cannot be ignored, nor can the damage done to humans' standing with God. Our own unintentional failures and deliberate acts, along with the scars and wounds we receive at the hands of others, can become like ghosts if they are ignored. And like horror-movie ghouls that have not been properly laid to rest, they one day wake up to take their revenge—sometimes many years, even decades later. So, as we focus once again on the final moments of Jesus on the cross, we look at the way in which forgiveness is supposed to work and at the wrong assumptions and unhelpful attitudes that can stop it from working.

A Powerful Example of Forgiveness

On Palm Sunday 2017, Naseem Faheem, the guard at St. Mark's Cathedral in Alexandria, redirected a suicide bomber who then detonated his bomb. Faheem was most likely the first to die in the blast but was responsible for saving the lives of many inside the church by redirecting the terrorist. When interviewed in their home, surrounded by children, Faheem's widow said she was telling the perpetrator that she wasn't angry at him but forgave him. The interviewer and his audience were stunned and marveled at her response. There were other reports of the Copts' astonishing offering of forgiveness.[1]

Orthodox priest Boules George addressed the terrorists while speaking to a congregation in Cairo: "I want to explain to you about our Christ. I want to tell you about how wonderful He is . . ." Then he said to the church: "How about we make a commitment to pray for them? Pray that they know the God of love? Pray that they experience the love of God? Because if they knew that God is love and experienced His love, they could not do these things—never, never, never."[2]

This powerful testimony shows that the Coptic Christians have learned the secret of how to forgive our enemies, but more than that, they have put into practice the teaching of Jesus that he shared with his disciples in Luke 7:47: "Whoever has been forgiven little loves little." In other words, Jesus is saying we cannot give to others what we've never received ourselves. If we've never received love, how can we give love to others? We cannot conjure up love by our own efforts or by the sheer force of our will. "Try harder" just doesn't work in real-life situations.

"My children need my forgiveness? How am I going to do it? I don't know, but I'll find a way, somehow I'm going to give it!"

"I don't care how much it hurts, I'm going to be nice to that person who betrayed me!"

"I'm supposed to love my neighbor? Okay. If I try hard enough, I will."

"My spouse needs my forgiveness? I don't know how, but I'm going to give it."

"I don't mind how painful it feels, or how much it hurts, I'm going to be kind to that person who intentionally betrayed my trust!"

So we try our very best. A frown on our face, teeth clenched. A quivering lip but a firm resolve: "I am going to forgive and love that person even if it nearly kills me!" But the Coptics didn't seem to be behaving in that manner. Perhaps somewhere along the line we are missing something? Perhaps the first step to forgiving and loving others is not *giving* love but *receiving*. The apostle John wrote: "We love because he first loved us" (1 John 4:19).

If you desire to love your enemy, a colleague who has wronged you, a friend who has let you down, John urges us to first accept Christ's love, and from that place will flow forgiveness and love for others.

Follow God's example, therefore, as dearly loved children and walk in the way of love, just as Christ loved us and gave himself up for us as a fragrant offering and sacrifice to God. (Eph. 5:1–2)

If you want to know the secret to forgiving others with a radical love like the Coptic Christians', you must first remember that you have been forgiven much.

We can then forgive each other, just as Christ forgave us. (Eph. 4:32 PAR)

We cannot love like this without God's help and assistance. It's impossible. A gracious spirit is not natural to our human sensibilities and is rarely found in our hearts. We cannot do it on our own; we must seek an alternative outside of ourselves. We need a transfusion of God's love into our hearts. To love the way God loves us means we must start by experiencing and receiving his love for us first.

Often we can be found guilty of skipping over the necessary first step of loving one another! We tell people to be patient in all situations, kind in every circumstance, and forgiving to all those who wrong them. But advising people to love without first receiving the revelation that God loves *them* is the equivalent of telling them to spend money on their credit cards without making a single deposit into their bank accounts.

Advising people to love without first receiving the revelation that God loves *them* is the equivalent of telling them to spend money on their credit cards without making a single deposit into their bank accounts.

It is not surprising then that relationships are strained. Relationships are in the red, overdrawn, and incurring debt and interest on a daily basis. People's output is greater than the input they receive and so they have insufficient funds and very little to give. In his first letter, the apostle John models and explains the right progression. He makes a significant input and deposit into the account before he tells us to swipe and use our credit card to withdraw.

First, the input:

> This is how God showed his love among us: He sent his one and
> only Son into the world that we might live through him. This
> is love: not that we loved God, but that he loved us and sent his
> Son as an atoning sacrifice for our sins." (1 John 4:9–10)

Then, having made such a weighty deposit, John implores us to get out our wallet and make a payment: "Dear friends, since God so loved us, we also ought to love one another" (v. 11). The secret to living loved is to be found in that forgotten first step that reflects many of our relationships.

I've recently been reflecting on Paul's prayer for the church community in Ephesus, for them to be "rooted and established in love" (Eph. 3:17). To draw from an agricultural metaphor, we are like a tree that needs to draw its nutrients from the soil found in good ground. If we are not replenished by remembering how loved and forgiven we are, we will not be established. That is where we draw our nourishment from—*knowing we are forgiven much and loved much.* If we do not hold on to this truth, we will be like a tree that is not planted in the soil—we won't grow, and our branches won't reach their full potential.

It is widely accepted and agreed that 1 Corinthians 13 is the most challenging and powerful chapter in the Bible. In my opinion, there are no other words that get to the heartbeat of what it means to love ourselves and to love others like the words packed into these few verses, particularly, verses 4–8:

> Love is patient, love is kind. It does not envy, it does not boast, it
> is not proud. It does not dishonor others, it is not self-seeking, it

is not easily angered, it keeps no record of wrongs. Love does not delight in evil but rejoices with the truth. It always protects, always trusts, always hopes, always perseveres. Love never fails.

I often reflect on these verses, almost as an inventory to see how well I am doing. They are like a mirror that reflects how well I am loving other people. Sometimes I put my name in the passage so it is easy to work out whether it was in fact truth or fiction: *"Ken is patient, Ken is kind. Ken does not envy, he does not boast, he is not proud . . ."*

These statements alone are enough! Ken is not always patient. Ken is not kind. Ask my wife and children. Ask my colleagues. Ask those closest to me. And for a long time that was my frustration with these verses and the command to live with this quality of love. It set such a high standard there was no way I could ever reach or attain it. I don't think anyone has the capacity to love in the way Paul described.

Of course, there is one—the man who turned Golgotha's hill of execution into a mount of transfiguration. The man who transformed death to life, hate to love, and pain to power. Jesus. He enables us to read 1 Corinthians 13 through a different lens. We see that this passage describes the abundant, limitless love of Jesus Christ.

Insert Jesus' name into various parts of 1 Corinthians 13:4–8, and it begins to carry weight: *"Jesus is patient, Jesus does not envy, Jesus is not proud. Jesus is not self seeking, Jesus is not easily angered. Jesus keeps no record of wrongs. Jesus always protects, Jesus always trusts, Jesus always hopes, Jesus always perseveres. Jesus never fails."*

Instead of letting this become a scripture that reminds us of our shortcomings and a standard of love we cannot produce in our own strength, we should let it draw us to a love we cannot resist nor replace, the love of God the Father, revealed to us through Jesus Christ. By his Spirit we are given the real power of "living love" in our everyday human interactions. It is the very starting point and place for our love for others. A love that was modeled to us by those Coptic Christians forgiving their persecutors.

Jesus didn't die alone on Golgotha. There were three crosses on the hill that day. If we consider the first cross to be "the cross of rejection," the second cross to be "the cross of repentance," and the third cross to be "the cross of redemption," then, in this story that I love very much, we will find illustrated everything we need to know about forgiveness.

The Cross of Rejection

One of the criminals who hung there on Golgotha said to Jesus, "Aren't you the Messiah? Save yourself and us!" (Luke 23:39). Maybe those of Jesus' disciples who had been there on Palm Sunday participating in the triumph and who were brave enough to follow him to Golgotha were quietly murmuring exactly the same challenge as this hardened criminal. Perhaps there was still a flicker of hope in their hearts that Jesus might, at the last minute, reach back into his Old Testament box of tricks, unleash the death angel or turn them all into pillars of salt, and then come down off the cross, smite the Roman overlords, and set his followers up as princes and rulers. But it is clear from the narrative that the criminal's question did not reflect this glimmer of hope, but was actually a cruel and well-aimed taunt.

Indeed, it is hard to overestimate how cruel this jibe was. Jesus was, after all, hanging on a cross, accused precisely of setting himself up as Israel's Messiah, whose central mission was to liberate Israel. The criminal, motivated perhaps by his own pain and anger, was poking at the open wound of Jesus' failed mission and identity. Nobody ever imagined a Messiah who would die on a cross, condemned as a criminal, apparently cursed by God. The Messiah was supposed to throw off the oppressor and bring freedom and vindication to God's people. It seems certain that Jesus was himself wrestling with precisely the question that the first criminal directed at him.

We share with the criminal this tendency to project our own fear and frustration onto Jesus. We tend to reduce him to the potential answer to whatever need is currently pressing in on us. It's as if we're saying to him, "Either you're my rescuer, saving me from my sins—or from illness, or redundancy, or pain—or you're nothing to me." This was the approach of the first criminal: rescue me or you are not who you claim to be.

When we, perhaps unintentionally, take this route, we see Jesus simply in light of what he might do for us. Our relationship with him becomes purely transactional. We might view him as a "genie" who can solve all our problems: "Save yourself and save us," as the first criminal stated it. Or we might imagine him as "celestial cashpoint," dealing out forgiveness, healing, and answers to prayer upon request. But if we just see Jesus in this mechanistic way, we cannot receive what he makes available to us.

And when we don't get what we want, we become angry. We want to gloss over our wrongdoings. Like the thief, we just want a miracle. We just want something to happen, for things to come right for us here and now. This kind of selfish short-termism is so typical of today's culture. I'm sure you can instantly recall many phone-in programs, with callers bemoaning their fate and demanding reparation. And there is definitely a sense of the criminal demanding that he be saved, taken care of, restored to the manner of life to which he would like to become accustomed, without any sense of taking responsibility or admitting fault.

We are a generation who is used to having everything we need and desire available on our mobile devices, the answer to any question at the swipe of a thumb or the tap of a finger. We literally have everything at our fingertips, and perhaps we are not willing to wait, to endure, and, dare I say it, to persevere. Instant gratification doesn't work when it comes to Jesus. We can only be saved when we recognize Jesus for who he is, show our repentance, and ask for forgiveness.

> **We can only be saved when we recognize Jesus for who he is, show our repentance, and ask for forgiveness.**

Recently, a woman from a Muslim background asked about the parable of the prodigal son. She clearly found it disturbing and was struggling with it. She wanted to know why the father loved one son—the bad, prodigal son, at that—more than his other son. Those of us who have grown up within Christianity are so used to reading the parable as a celebration of the gracious love of the father for the prodigal son that it never occurs to us that someone coming from another religious tradition might find it offensive. But, of course, the offense is mistaken. The love of the father is not lacking in any way. He loves both his sons equally, with a burning love beyond our comprehension. The question is whether the sons are in a position to receive that love.

By the close of the parable, the younger son is in a position to receive the love of the father because he has recognized his failure and his need. Because he opens himself up, the father is able to pour out his love upon him—signified by the ring, the robe, and the great feast. The older son, however, is proud. He'd like the ring, the robe, and the feast, but in his hauteur, he is not open to the love that those things represent. Ironically, he is making exactly the same mistake at the end of the parable as his younger brother made at the beginning: *he wants to receive the rewards without the relationship*. He wants to take what he can from his father but without the responsibility of examining and sharing his own life.

The Danish philosopher Soren Kierkegaard reflected at length on the puzzling fact that many of those who lived and worked, walked and talked alongside Jesus never recognized him for who he truly is. The first criminal was not alone in encountering Jesus and completely missing the point. In the chapter "The Case of the Contemporary Disciple," in the book *The Portable Kierkegaard*, the narrator puts words into the mouth of such a first-century contemporary of Jesus:

> I ate and drank in his presence, and he taught in our streets. I saw him often, and knew him for a common man of humble origin. Only a very few thought to find something extraordinary in him; as far as I am concerned, I could see nothing remarkable about him, and I was certainly as much of a contemporary as anybody.[3]

This appears to have been the experience of the first criminal. Even confronted with Jesus upon the cross, he could recognize nothing remarkable in him. Kierkegaard, however, actually takes encouragement from this strange fact. If even contemporaries who could see and hear and touch Jesus could only *recognize* him by the grace of God, then we who live two thousand years later are in exactly the same position as those contemporaries. We can only see Jesus and know Jesus as he reveals himself to us.

> "The Teacher" was not immediately knowable; he could be known only when he himself gave the condition. Whoever received the condition received it from the Teacher himself, and hence the Teacher must know everyone who knows him, and no one can know the Teacher except through being known by him.[4]

If we are to receive the forgiveness made available by Jesus' death on the cross, we must allow the Holy Spirit to reveal Jesus for who he truly is, not just for what he can do for us. Further, we must be willing to see ourselves as we truly are. We may consider ourselves to be completely different from the first criminal, but are we?

The Cross of Repentance

The criminal hanging on the second cross is remarkable. We see that, while God is not so moved by our demands or our anger or our railing against him, he is profoundly moved by our sorrowful repentance. A very important interchange takes place here. One of the criminals who hung there hurled insults at him:

> "Aren't you the Messiah? Save yourself and us!" But the other criminal rebuked him. "Don't you fear God," he said, "since you are under the same sentence? We are punished justly, for we are getting what our deeds deserve. But this man has done nothing wrong." Then he said, "Jesus, remember me when you

come into your kingdom." Jesus answered him, "Truly I tell you, today you will be with me in paradise." (Luke 23:39–43)

Unlike the first criminal, the second criminal addressed Jesus by name: "Jesus, remember me when you come into your kingdom" (v. 42). We know from the Old Testament prophecies of Joel and from Paul's New Testament letter to the church in Rome that "everyone who calls on the name of the Lord will be saved" (Rom. 10:13). And the apostle Peter made the same point in his sermon recorded in the book of Acts, when he declared, "Salvation is found in no one else, for there is no other name under heaven given to mankind by which we must be saved" (4:12).

It seems that the second criminal was somehow aware of this fact. He had come to the realization, we know not how, that the name of Jesus was the saving name. His gaze was focused on Jesus. He appeared not to hear the baying of the crowd. He appeared unmoved by the taunts of the other criminal. Is the same thing not true today? When we catch a glimpse of who Jesus truly is, when we get a sense of his relentless love, everything else fades into the background.

When we catch a glimpse of who Jesus truly is, when we get a sense of his relentless love, everything else fades into the background.

Having recognized Jesus for who he truly is, the second criminal also gained insight into his own life and situation. In this extraordinary interchange, with words forced out between gasps for breath and grimaces of pain, the second criminal said to his neighbor: "Don't you fear God since you are under the same sentence?" (Luke 23:40).

Drawing attention to the contrast between the justice of the sentences they had received and the enormous injustice of Jesus' position, he continued: "We are punished justly, for we are getting what our deeds deserve. But this man has done nothing wrong" (v. 41). It is the most amazing statement to find on the lips of a man suffering torture and dying. In this one sentence he believed, he repented, he confessed, he preached, he trusted, he loved, he prayed. All in one sentence. The first person truly to understand what it is to be justified by faith in Jesus Christ alone was a robber on a cross.

If you ever want to know what repentance really is, you can do no better than to meditate on that sentence. Read it, repeat it, and apply it to your own life and situation. We must name our sin so that we can claim God's mercy. In this brief exclamation, we can recognize an appropriate fear of God, by which I mean an overwhelming awe-filled sense of love and respect for him—a recognition that we don't deserve his favor and a recognition that our misdeeds stand between us and him.

> The first person truly to understand what it is to be justified by faith in Jesus Christ alone was a robber on a cross.

Luther's biographer noted: "Every sin in order to be absolved, was to be confessed. Therefore the soul must be searched and the memory ransacked and the motives probed."[5] When was the last time you searched your soul, ransacked your memory, or probed your motives? Just as a half-hearted confession will result in a half-hearted sense of forgiveness, a specific confession will result in a more assured state of having been forgiven.

And yet we are caught off guard by how our contemporary culture defines sin. The waves of moral relativism have swept our shores, and "No moral absolutes!" is the cry from the rooftops of our society. Many today view God's commandments as draconian, intolerant, and unthinkable. If we cannot rightly identify sin for what it is, how is it possible for us to identify, uphold, and defend what Jesus taught, in his proper context of love? Moreover, if we cannot rightly identify and define sin and take it seriously, then how can we wholeheartedly turn from it in our moments of repentance? After all, if I don't see speaking ill of others as a sin or telling a lie as a sin, how can I be forgiven? If no sin means no forgiveness, we have deprived ourselves of what we most need.

The criminal continued, "Jesus, remember me when you come into your kingdom" (v. 42). It's likely that the criminal's hope was for some indeterminate time in the future, some far distant resurrection of the dead. Isn't it amazing that Jesus takes this vague hope and turns it into a promise of immediate relief? "Today you will be with me in paradise." This is the glory of repentance, that we can receive forgiveness in the very moment that we request it. Jesus is the one who can forgive us, and remarkably he wants to forgive us today.

"Today," Jesus says to you and me. You don't have to wait for the circumstances to be right before you come to Jesus. You don't have to clean yourself up, sort out your life, prepare the way. If a criminal suffering and dying on a cross could turn to Jesus and receive his forgiveness, you don't have to sort out your life, fix up a job, embark on a relationship, wait until you're in a better place, develop your prayer life, or otherwise prettify yourself. No, you can come to Jesus today. Right now, you can hear his words of forgiveness and hope, your own version of the promise he gave to the dying criminal: "Today, you will be with me in paradise."

I was once asked out to lunch by a friend of mine who is one of the most successful investors in the city. We met at a very well-known and expensive restaurant. What was totally unexpected was the content of our conversation. He asked me about God. I could hardly believe it! After all, nothing in my knowledge of him suggested that he would be remotely interested in God. I stammered away talking about God and how he was revealed in the person of Jesus. After this conversation, he started to read and think more about Jesus and came to a real faith in him. I felt convicted for having such false assumptions about a man for whom Jesus died.

My friend took his new faith seriously and started building a new life, which intrigued and puzzled his friends in the financial world. His first action on coming to faith was to restore the fractured relationships he had with his family members, and he then set out to apply his new faith to the way he lived, worked, and carried out his relationships. I was humbled and amazed by his energy and determination to live this new life. But what really stung was when he said to me, "I never knew that forgiveness could be so powerful. I feel totally freed up. Why did you not tell me this before?" He had found true hope in Jesus' offer of total forgiveness. But what was this hope built upon? We can only understand if we look to the third cross, the one on which Jesus died.

The Cross of Redemption

The cross was the place where Jesus took upon himself everything that separates us from God, everything that keeps us from abundant life in the presence of God. It is on the third cross that the toll of sin is taken care of, the relationship between God and us is restored and repaired, the bridge is built, and an extraordinary new life is made available. The third cross is the cross of redemption.

I recently came across a rather interesting reality program:

Barter Kings. It instantly grabbed my attention, as it's all about trading. The premise of the program is that you trade something of lesser value for something of greater value. If you do it enough times, you end up with something of significant value. For example, you start with a pencil and trade it for a used set of headphones, then trade the used set of headphones for an iPad, trade the iPad for an around-the-world airplane ticket, the airplane ticket for a mortgage on a house, and then the mortgage on a house for a cul-de-sac of houses. Voila!

The show tracks those trading deals, and it's full of unexpected twists and turns. One of the most infamous trading strings involved a Canadian blogger who started with a single paper clip. It took nearly a year and fourteen peculiar transactions. By the time he was done, the paper clip was traded all the way up to a farmhouse. An incredibly radical exchange! But not as radical as the exchange that happens and is won for us on the cross.

"God made him who had no sin to be sin for us, so that in him we might become the righteousness of God" (2 Cor. 5:21). Here's the trade deal the "Barter King" puts on the table: you trade all your sin and mistakes for all his righteousness, and he calls it even. You'll never get a better deal. And that's why it's called the good news. Salvation is the greatest exchange ever known.

What Jesus Christ did on the cross was to carry out this glorious exchange. John Calvin called it the wondrous exchange. He took all our failures and shortcomings upon himself and exchanged them. He took the ugly brutality of our lives and exchanged it for the beautiful. He took the sin of our lives and exchanged it for our salvation. He took the meaninglessness of our lives and exchanged it for purpose. He took the mistakes of our lives and exchanged them for gifts and callings.

Many of the words we use to describe Jesus' actions on the cross are taken from the commercial world. Exchange is at the center of financial transactions. We talk of swapping one liability for a better opportunity. Bonds are redeemed when they reach their maturity dates. What then is the exchange rate of the cross? All our sin is transferred to Christ's account. All his righteousness is transferred to our account. He took the rejection we have received at the hands of others and the rejection we have meted out, and he exchanged it for restored relationship. It was not nails but love that held God to a cross.

At the cross, he took off his robe and put on our sin, so that we could wear his righteousness. I deserved punishment and got forgiveness. I deserved wrath and got love. Philip Yancey said, "I deserved a debtor's prison and got instead a clean credit history. I deserved stern lectures and crawl-on-your-knees repentance; I got a banquet—Babette's feast—spread for me."[6]

> **It was not nails but love that held God to a cross.**

In the film *Face Off*, the main character, played by Nicholas Cage, takes his face off through surgery and puts it on an agent so that the agent can move through the crowd with the face of an innocent man. Similarly, Jesus has done his own "face off," of epic proportions. It is as if he says, "I will cover your sins so well and I'll make you look so much like me that, when you go to the Father, you can go as me!" "And I will do whatever you ask in my name" (John 14:13). Salvation is a face off, and if you've been living life shame-faced, God says, "I've got another face for you. I'll put it on you now. And just as I became evil for you, you will become righteous for me." It is the righteousness of God.

Jesus bent his will to the mystery of suffering and walked

headlong into the painful persecution of men, even men who knew not what they did. He suffered the intense pain of having his identity—the essence of who he was—attacked by people with rigid and systematic notions of God. The Jewish leaders considered themselves defenders of the faith, of right theology. The Roman guards were quellers of insurrection and uprising. And Jesus was stuck between two groups of people with very different and very strong personal opinions, like a garment being stretched to ripping.

"Father, forgive them, for they do not know what they are doing" (Luke 23:34). His last words were a prayer. He could have prayed, "Father, forgive them their sins." After all, he forgave others their sins. Had he meant, "Forgive them their sins," though, he would have prayed it. Instead, the connotation seems different, *more gentle*. Jesus recognized that they were *unknowing*. Instead, I wonder whether the phrase may be read with more human intuition: *Father, forgive them—they are doing the best they know how*. And by placing ourselves within the loving mercy of these words, we are released with the most extraordinary grace.

> At the cross there is the strangest and most beautiful encounter—a once-for-all meeting of human beings at their worst and God at his best.

We have encountered here the beauty of cruciform love, an agony of beauty, which emerges in the midst of the greatest ugliness, like poppies on corpse-strewn Flanders fields. At the cross there is the strangest and most beautiful encounter—a once-for-all meeting of human beings at their worst and God at his best. And it is here, and like this, that God forgives his world.

A Time to Meditate

Music

- "Beautiful Exchange," Joel Houston, Hillsong United
- "Farewell to Stromness," Peter Maxwell Davies

Reflect

- The first criminal railed and raged. "Save yourself and save us," he said to Jesus. As if Jesus were a kind of celestial cashpoint, dealing out solutions of our choosing on request. But he missed the point. And he missed out on the relationship. Today we can say to Jesus, "I want you more than I want solutions" and wait to see what happens.
- Remember that Jesus was immediately able to forgive the second criminal because of his genuine and sorrowful repentance. The criminal named his wrongdoing and recognized Jesus for who he was. Now I encourage you to do the same. And you, too, will hear him say, "Truly I tell you, today you will be with me in paradise." Today! Forgiveness is instant.
- Calvin used the phrase "the wondrous exchange." Now is a great moment to ask God to bring to mind anything ugly you'd like to be rid of—failures, shortcomings, bad attitudes, messed-up relationships—and in repentance and gratitude, ask Jesus to exchange

them for his righteousness. Ugliness for beauty. Let the exchange take place and dwell on the extraordinary truth that you now have a restored and renewed relationship with God.

Prayer

Lord, how can I thank you for what you have done for me on the cross? Thank you that you have exchanged my sins for salvation and my meaninglessness for purpose. Give me a humble heart to receive your forgiveness and a grateful heart to know that I am now—today—clothed in your righteousness, amen.

FIVE

FRIENDSHIP

Therefore, if anyone is in Christ, the new creation has come: The old has gone, the new is here! All this is from God, who reconciled us to himself through Christ and gave us the ministry of reconciliation: that God was reconciling the world to himself in Christ, not counting people's sins against them. And he has committed to us the message of reconciliation. We are therefore Christ's ambassadors, as though God were making his appeal through us. We implore you on Christ's behalf: Be reconciled to God. God made him who had no sin to be sin for us, so that in him we might become the righteousness of God.

—2 Corinthians 5:17–21

I HAVE TITLED THIS CHAPTER "FRIENDSHIP" IN THE hope of encapsulating what sweetness awaits us all when we are reconciled with God through his forgiveness. When we put our faith in Jesus Christ, we are not simply forgiven and left alone to our own devices. Instead, we enter an entirely different dimension with God—a relationship with God himself. It is a relationship that is predicated upon Jesus' forgiveness of our sins. After Jesus had done all that his Father asked of him during his thirty-three years on earth, he was reunited with his Father. The reunion that Jesus experienced enabled us, too, to become a part of that reunion and to come back into friendship with the Father.

This truth was illuminated to me when I asked Professor David Ford, the Emeritus Regius Professor of Theology at the University of Cambridge and the author of a soon-to-be-published commentary on John's Gospel, what the key idea was in John. He replied that he was not sure of the key idea, because there were many to choose from, but he was sure about the key word: it was *friend*. Jesus says, "No longer do I call you servants . . . but I have called you friends, for all that I have heard from my Father I have made known to you" (John 15:15 ESV). Everything Jesus knew of his heavenly Father he has made known to you and me. To put it another way, Jesus has confided in us. It is as if Jesus has made us sharers in the family secrets of the Trinity. What a privilege that we are not just the subjects of Jesus' work on the cross but are now his friends.

Jesus, the Light of the World, by William Holman Hunt, is one of my favorite paintings. It hangs in St. Paul's Cathedral and often, when working nearby, I would go and sit and stare at it for a while and let the extraordinary intimacy of the painting seep into me. It helped soften the hard edges that would so often build up after weeks and months of office life.

The painting is taken from Revelation 3:20: "Behold, I stand at the door, and knock: if any man hear my voice, and open the door, I will come in to him, and will sup with him, and he with me" (KJV). I love these words. If I choose to open the door of my heart to Jesus, he will "come in and sup with me." Two people sharing a meal was a sign of deep intimacy in the culture of the time. To share a meal with Jesus, metaphorically speaking, assumes a very real and trusting friendship. And this is what he offers so gently and without force, if only we dare to open the door to him.

Some years ago that painting was sent out for cleaning. When the restorer took off the mounting, he found words painted under the frame by Hunt, written for no one to see but himself. They were written to the One behind the painting: "Forgive me Lord Jesus that I kept you waiting so long."

Jesus stands at the door and knocks and wants to establish a friendship with us. But what exactly do I mean by *friendship*? I think of it as a reciprocal relationship between two people, and that is all God wanted for us from the very beginning of time, when he created the earth.

We see in Genesis exactly what God had in mind: Adam and Eve, newly created, enjoyed an incredibly close, intimate friendship with God—a friendship without religion, regulations, rituals, or rigmarole. In fact, there weren't any rules other than the command not to eat from the tree of knowledge. They could do everything else, but God commanded them to obey that one rule. The Bible says that Adam and Eve delighted in God, and he delighted in them. That is the way God wanted to establish a friendship with humanity. Adam and Eve, as our representatives, were made to live in constant friendship with God and in his continual presence.

That ideal, however, was ruined by sin and disobedience. Sin broke the friendship. Adam and Eve's mistake ruptured the glorious state of union between themselves and God. It would only be through the cross of Jesus that humankind could once again find and establish a renewed, reconciled friendship with God. It is a friendship that is of eternal importance because, as my friend Rick Warren often says, "Loving and knowing God is our greatest privilege, and being known and loved by God is our greatest pleasure."[1]

How can we make this reconciling fellowship of the cross part of the fabric of our everyday lives at home, in the workplace, in our friendships, in our families as we care for young children and older relatives, and in responding to the poor and marginalized? How can we mirror the extraordinary grace and friendship God has shown to us? To an estranged family member, a hurt friend, warring colleagues? In the same way that we can find ourselves resisting the offer of reconciliation with God, we can also shrink from the challenge of restoring our relationships with other people. I know, as I'm sure you do, that friendships can be testing at times, yet we are called to resolve conflict and to reconcile strained or broken relationships.

God was so deeply committed to restoring friendship with Adam and Eve that he didn't abandon them in the garden; instead, he decided on a new route to reconcile them with himself. In car navigation systems, if the driver does not follow the directions given by the navigator—turning, for instance, left instead of right—the navigator traces a new route, beginning from the new position and reaching the desired destination in a different way. This is what God did with humankind, deciding that he would put his plan of redemption into operation through the cross.

It follows then, that for us to experience this restored and renewed friendship, we must first pass through the cross of Christ. After all, by sinning, humanity contracted a debt with God that was too big a price for us to pay. Christ at the cross had to fight against the forces of evil that held us as slaves to sin and separated us from friendship with him (Heb. 2:14–15).

I find it interesting that Paul wrote, "Christ Jesus, *Himself human*" (1 Tim. 2:5 HCSB, emphasis added). This reminds us that, in order for God to mediate on our behalf, Jesus had to identify with our humanity. He was able to represent us because he became one of us, yet was without sin. And so the reconciliation between God and humanity was achieved.

This was the ultimate sacrifice, the one perfect sacrifice, which exceeds the logic of the Old Testament; year after year people placed their hands (and thus their sins) onto the sacrificial animal, which was then killed—and thus, their sins with it. But, of course, this could only ever be a picture, as "it is impossible for the blood of bulls and goats to take away sins" (Heb. 10:4). It became clear that humankind could not atone for everyone's sin by the high priest's sacrifice on the Day of Atonement once a year. There needed to be an ultimate sacrifice, someone who could forgive people of their sins, once and for all.

Jesus' coming reversed this mechanism, as it is no longer humanity looking for ways to pay the price of sin through the Old Testament sacrifice of animals, but it is God himself carrying on his own shoulders the sins of the whole world. Jesus' suffering on the cross, his death, and his resurrection have opened a way to the overwhelming joy of reconciliation, which, of course, is utterly undeserved.

Blessed Are the Peacemakers

It is in light of this that we, as followers of Jesus, are called to be agents of reconciliation and bringers of peace in every area of our lives. Indeed, Jesus said, in his penultimate beatitude in Matthew's Gospel, "Blessed are the peacemakers, for they will be called children of God" (Matt. 5:9). We are shown to be children of God, who are maturing in our friendship with God, if we are peacemakers. It is the mark of our faith.

To be a peacemaker means to have grace-healed eyes that see the potential in others to receive the same grace that God has so lavishly bestowed on us. All those who want to be messengers of reconciliation must be ready to abandon the "cause-and-effect program" instituted by the world and to embrace freely God's "grace program." When we do so, we become Christ's ambassadors in a world filled with people who need the grace that God freely offers. Being reconciled to God, and showing others the way to a right relationship with their Maker, is not about what we do but about what God has done through Christ.

It is important to note that being a peacemaker does not mean avoiding or appeasing. We are not called to ignore things, nor are we to avoid causing problems so that we can get along with one another. Jesus never ran from a legitimate conflict, but rather he knew how to deal with it head-on, resolve it, and restore the relationship. This is a world rife with conflict: between nations and within nations, between generations, races, religions, political parties, the sexes. It is a world of struggle and misunderstanding between cultures, between rich and poor, educated and uneducated. We desperately need peacemakers in our world, and we need to be peacemakers in our own lives.

It is for this reason that I am motivated by my work as the chairman of the Archbishop of Canterbury's Reconciling Leaders Network, which is designed to train and teach leaders in reconciliation—how to build bridges amid dividing opinions and what can oftentimes be hostile environments to lead in. On a far larger scale, this is what we see Desmond Tutu, the anti-apartheid and human rights activist in South Africa, accomplishing in his own lifetime and ministry. When I had the privilege of meeting him, he struck me as one of the great leaders of our time—a man who has made relational reconciliation his priority, with his whole focus on bringing people together in a world that is both hostile and dangerous.

It is the death of Jesus that provides us with the opportunity and the ability to be peacemakers. The message of the cross was never meant to be some exclusive, insider deal for private Christian consumption. No, the message of the cross was to be a signpost showing everybody the way to this extraordinary friendship.

Regardless of gender, race, and nationality, the cross of Jesus is a message of hope for all who accept and put their faith in him.

Regardless of gender, race, and nationality, the cross of Jesus is a message of hope for all who accept and put their faith in him. Jesus took no shortcuts on the cross, and the new, restored friendship that he established is powerful enough to overcome any and every obstacle.

Friendship Restored

As Jesus made his journey to the cross to enable the friendship between God and humanity to be restored in its entirety, he experienced the trials of human friendship as, one after another, his disciples let him down. Judas betrayed him for thirty pieces of silver. In his hour of need at Gethsemane, his friends fell asleep. Peter then disowned him three times, denying not only that he was his friend but that he had ever known him. Of course, one can only be betrayed by a friend; an enemy cannot betray you.

To rebuild relationships after such disappointment and ill treatment required something extraordinary. But Peter's friendship was fully restored when he met Jesus again. The memory of the crowing cock no longer became an agonizing trigger of his conscience. Instead, he knew the sweetness of a fully restored relationship with his close friend. Judas never reached out to try to restore the friendship. His betrayal was complete, and the trigger of his conscience led to his suicide.

Friendship happens when mercy wins over justice. The cross was a victory of love, and every day we're to take up that cross of love and follow his example of sacrifice and mercy in our own lives.

I am amazed at Jesus, in an act of utter obedience, voluntarily going to the cross. Whereas he interrupted Abraham from sacrificing his son Isaac, God stayed quiet when Jesus was on the cross. The Father suffered with the Son. But that wasn't the end of the story, because God the Father raised Jesus from the grave. That victory and truth is central because it shows us the love and friendship engrained in this Trinitarian act of God.

We are told that "if we walk in the light,

Friendship happens when mercy wins over justice.

as he is in the light, we have fellowship with one another, and the blood of Jesus, his Son, purifies us from all sin" (1 John 1:7). Reconciliation became active at the cross and works in us through the Holy Spirit. "And with that he breathed on them and said, 'Receive the Holy Spirit'" (John 20:22). Through the cross, the Spirit creates a new state of relational reconciliation and gives us the power to live by it in a fractured world.

The ultimate source of reconciliation and unity is found in the Trinity. Unlike other polytheistic religions that speak of divinity in a permanent state of rivalry and war among themselves, the Trinity exists in a relationship of perfect interdependent self-giving love. Archbishop Justin Welby said, "We change our conflicted communities when we rediscover reconciliation in Christ for ourselves."[2] We have a responsibility to be the church of Christ, and we should, therefore, look like the Christ who founded the church. We should look like reconcilers.

Archbishop Welby continued: "Paul reminds the divided Ephesians that God breaks down all barriers. They are reconciled through the cross to God and are to be reconciled to others."[3] This kind of healing is not simple or easy; it is painful. We live in a culture where the focus is on self, and we are not immune from the temptations of prestige, position, and popularity. The ego resists taking the initiative in reconciling with other people. But we have been called to be different, to resist the old world order. And being different means taking the initiative.

We have been called to mirror our own Savior, Jesus Christ, who reached down and took the initiative for us. Amid conflict and fractured relationships, amid disagreements and disdain, the resurrection of Christ has ushered in a new creation, where we can live and respond in a different way. This is the nature of this strange kingdom: a kingdom in which we can be agents for change, as the resurrection gives us a glimpse into the new world order, one in which we can work toward reconciliation and unity.

We are to be part of a new empowered community, living in the midst of the old world order, a community that loves and cares for others amid our differences in the most radical and Christlike way. The message of Jesus whispers an invitation, beckoning us to "come and follow," allowing his love to redirect us so that we might play our part in revitalizing our world.

And the world can, strangely, be revitalized by the life of just one person. I think, inevitably, of Nelson Mandela, whom I had the great joy to meet when I was a trustee of the Mandela Children's Fund in the United Kingdom. As we met, I found myself wondering how he did it. How did he find the energy to forgive after such profound injustice, such terrible personal suffering? How did he emerge with so little bitterness in his heart?

There is a story of a young activist who was brought to Robben Island. He was full of rage about the conditions of the prison and kept saying to the other prisoners, "I will get revenge on the warden. I will break him, as he breaks us." When Mandela heard about this, he called the man in, sat him down, and said, "If you do this, you'll be as bad as them and we are better. You cannot live with bitterness. It will eat you up each day. Learn to forgive instead."[4]

What makes a response like Mandela's possible? I was given a clue on a recent trip to the Vatican, when I had the privilege of joining with a small group on a visit to Pope Francis. As we prepared for our visit, we prayed together. The leader of the group said, "We should wash each other's feet." At this point, I thought to myself, *No one has ever washed my feet and I've never washed anyone else's.* But the leader spoke a great truth to us: "If you want to have reconciliation, you must start with the feet first. Not the head in debate, nor the heart in empathy, but with the feet. If you start with feet you will reach the head and heart."

It is through the act of washing feet, through humbling ourselves and serving others that we are charged with the energy and resources to forgive. Mandela epitomized this in his response to apartheid, and it's a model for us. When we need to forgive and be reconciled to each other, we start from a posture of humility. We seek the best interest of the other person, while remaining true and sincere to our own personal convictions, without compromise, and without demoralizing the other person. It might seem counter-cultural, but therein lies the answer.

A Community of Reconciliation

For the Christian, the energy to live differently comes from the cross of Christ, where hatred was exchanged for love, revenge for forgiveness, isolation for unity, enmity for reconciliation. In that glorious exchange a new community emerges: a community that draws strength and energy from the cross of Jesus Christ; a community in which human beings, reconciled to God through the cross, have the power to be reconciled to each other.

My son broke his arm when sledding down a hill many years ago. I remember the doctor telling him, as he bound his arm in a cast, that it wouldn't be long before his left arm, the one that was broken, would be stronger than his right. If a broken bone is properly set, it knits together. But it can only knit together in something that is alive. The bones of dead people don't knit together! But in the case of a living person, where there is a fracture and a break, there is also vitality, aliveness—energy. Yes, at the end of the process you may remember the break, and there may even be a ridge or a mark where that breach occurred. But when healing has taken place, the reknit bone is strongest *at the very point of the fracture.* And as it is in the human body, so it is with the Spirit of God.

God strengthens our friendships at the very point of their fracture. The Holy Spirit is released, by Jesus' death and resurrection, to knit our brokenness and to restore our friendships. If we walk with the Spirit long enough—responding to his prompting, his values, and his voice—then his vision becomes ours. St. Augustine famously prayed, "Grant what you command, and command what you wish,"[5] and his prayer truly understood the ways of the Lord. For God does command holiness, repeatedly saying, "Be holy as I am holy." But the holiness he calls for is the holiness he provides, as, by the power of the Spirit, he enables us to conform to his commands and to be transformed into the likeness of Jesus.

Holiness comes to the extent that we walk with and work with the gift of the Holy Spirit. The very places where we feel weakest, where we have allowed fissures to develop, or where catastrophic breakdowns in relationship have isolated us, there the Spirit is able to make us strong. Just as the broken bone can be restored to be stronger than ever, so our friendship can be remade—deeper and truer than before.

This is the boundless energy of the reconciling God, which is released by Christ's work on the cross. And the person who cannot forgive has forgotten how much they have been forgiven. Philip Yancey wrote, "Left alone, cracks widen, and for the resulting chasms of un-grace there is only one remedy: the bridge of forgiveness between people,"[6] which is modeled and enabled by the redeeming bridge of the cross.

A friend told me about the pioneering work of a charity in Israel called Sport for Peace, in which sports teams made up of a mix of children of both Arab and Jewish cultures compete in football, rugby, even Frisbee. The fun and the fellowship are far more important than the competition, and relationships across the cultural and religious divide thrive. This may not immediately herald longed-for peace in the Palestinian–Israeli conflict, but it is one of a number of small statements of reconciliation that will begin to bring hope to cultures and communities that have suffered devastating loss over the centuries of division. These are the bridges across which the gospel truth travels.

Broken Things Made Whole

We must follow Christ for ourselves, but we can't follow Christ by ourselves. True Christlike community holds diversity within unity, like the Trinity through which it is empowered. Confrontations and complications may (and almost certainly will) arise as a by-product, but, as we choose love, we can become more together than we could ever be by ourselves. N. T. Wright said,

> Our task, as image-bearing, God-loving, Christ-shaped, Spirit-filled Christians, following Christ and shaping our world, is to announce redemption to a world that has discovered its fallenness, to announce healing to a world that has discovered its brokenness, to proclaim love and trust to a world that knows only exploitation, fear and suspicion.[7]

Our lives and actions must bear witness to the cross and

resurrection, demonstrating that God's kingdom, strange as it may seem, really has been launched on earth as it is in heaven.

Kintsugi, also known as "golden repair," is the Japanese art of taking broken items made of ceramics, glass, or other material and repairing them using gold lacquer in such a way that a new vessel is formed. As a philosophy, the process treats breakage and repair as part of the history of the object, rather than as something to disguise or hide. The life and function of the object does not end at the moment of breakage or damage; in fact, this is just the beginning of it being reformed into something new and even more beautiful.[8]

The analogy is powerful in the context of our friendship with Jesus. As individuals, our flaws and mistakes are refashioned by God and, in a process of golden repair, they are remade into something even more valuable. In the corporate context, broken relationships or damaged friendships can be refashioned and rebuilt into something stronger and longer lasting.

The restored item, say a bowl, is displayed with its gold-filled fractures. What a picture of the work of the Spirit as he comes to heal the fissures of our lives, particularly after a shattering experience of illness, bereavement, loss of employment, breakdown in a relationship, depression, and despair. Through the intense and sometimes seemingly unbearable pain, and through the healing power of God, life can become even more beautiful than it was before the shattering event.

The Holy Spirit wants to form a church that is to be a friendship-based colony of heaven. "The world at its worst needs the church at its best."[9] But before we can make a change in society, God has got to make a change in us. Before we can be out there presenting the change-giving gospel to others, we've got to be changed by it ourselves. We need to know that we have an extraordinary friendship with Jesus. It is then that we become bearers of the amazing news that everyone is invited to come just as they are.

You don't have to put on some religious garb or clothe yourself in a whole new set of philosophies or a whole new set of habits. You are who you are—whatever your circumstances, whatever your history, whatever your damage, whatever your pain—and you are loved and welcomed by God, just as I am who I am, and I am loved by God. He wants to use every single one of us to form this strange, upside-down kingdom where broken things are made whole. To show faith in the gospel is not merely theological accuracy but also relational unity. And relational unity is not about how well we impress each other, but how well we inconvenience ourselves for one another, modeling ourselves after our Savior and Friend, Jesus Christ. What a strange kingdom it is when we, the subjects, become friends with the King. Or, as the old hymn says: "What a friend we have in Jesus!"[10]

He wants to use every single one of us to form this strange, upside-down kingdom where broken things are made whole.

And so I find myself asking, Am I living a life that only makes sense in the light of the resurrection? Am I living a life where my relationships are of such a quality that they don't make sense if this life is all there is? What is the answer for you? After all, our friendship with God has huge implications for our relationships with others, which will in turn be shaped by our view of where this whole story is leading. To help bring in the kingdom, we have something to do here on earth. We must proactively follow the way of reconciliation and forgiveness, the way of the cross.

The more indifferent we become to seeking God's reconciling power, the less God's power will make any difference in our lives. And so may we join together in praying for a greater outpouring of his Spirit, which would bring with it a supernatural strengthening of the bonds of reconciliation between human beings here on earth, and between humanity and our God.

A Time to Meditate

Music

- "Mercy," Matt Redman
- "Hymn of the Cherubim," Tchaikovsky

Reflect

- Jesus stands at the door of your heart and he knocks. In the stillness and silence of this moment, can you hear him? To those who open the door, he will come in and "sup with you." This is quite a moment. Quite an offer. Quite a guest. Will you invite him in?
- Loving and knowing God is our greatest privilege, and being loved and known by God is our greatest pleasure. Friendship with God means friendship with each other, as we are set free to love others with and through his love. This is a good moment to ask the Holy Spirit to breathe his healing power on any

broken relationships, and to breathe his life on all your relationships.

- Now take a moment, if you'd like, to ask the Holy Spirit to come and heal the fissures of your life—the places where you've been shattered. And picture God's process of golden repair, the bowl with its gold-filled fractures making it even more beautiful. This is you.

Prayer

Lord, I thank you that through Christ's victory on the cross, I can know the sweet intimacy of a friendship with you. And that through that friendship broken bonds can be restored and new life breathed into my relationship with you and with others, amen.

SIX

FREEDOM

For through the law, I died to the law that I might live for God. I have been crucified with Christ and I no longer live, but Christ lives in me. The life I now live in the body, I live by faith in the Son of God, who loved me and gave himself for me.

—Galatians 2:19–20

I CONFESS THAT FEW TEXTS IN THE NEW TESTAMENT

have been as puzzling to me as this one, and yet, at the same time, as liberating. Over the years, I have reflected again and again on these seemingly paradoxical words. I have been crucified with Christ? Me? We hear preachers talking about the need to "die with Christ," but what on earth are they talking about? Where is the good news? For me to be fully alive, I have to die? Where is the freedom in that?

The longing for freedom is deeply ingrained in all our lives. I lived the earlier part of my life in a country where freedom was severely curtailed; the prevailing corrupted belief was that racial segregation was the foundation of true freedom, and countless lives were lost to that end each day. When I left South Africa and came to study in England, the contrast was striking. I had come from a tinderbox atmosphere, unrest bubbling under the surface of life, and here was total ease; here was freedom. But was it true freedom? The freedom for which Christ died for us?

Mostly we picture freedom in political terms: those vivid pictures of the crumbling Berlin Wall and the release of Nelson Mandela. But the freedom we can enjoy as Christians goes far deeper, existing within the complex terrain of each human heart and yielding great fruit. It's the freedom to experience a new life "living for God" (v. 19), and in this chapter I want to explore what that freedom *really* looks like. Is it possible that we can be free from having to live according to the prevailing philosophy, which claims that personal gain is our priority? And what of the ravages of sin around our ankles, which can slow us down or even bring us to a complete halt? Can this freedom we hear of in the New Testament truly release us from all of this?

I have a contemporary sculpture of Jesus Christ in my study. The Christ figure is depicted as if he is on the cross—the face in agony, the crown of thorns evident, the nail wounds visible—but his hands are lifted high above his head. It is as if he is reaching up, resurrected, while still on the cross.

I remember a young man we'll call Dan, who had come looking for advice, sitting with me in my study. He was facing redundancy, and he felt overwhelmed by fear about his future. More than anything, he just wanted control. He wanted his finances, his career trajectory, his professional status—all of it—to be in exactly the right place. And now this possible redundancy threatened to undermine the building blocks he had so carefully established in his life. He was in a state of great anxiety and felt that everything—even his faith—was under threat. We turned and looked at the sculpture in my study as we talked and prayed, and I asked him where and how he saw himself in relation to the Christ figure.

From the experience of my own life and from observing the lives of others over many years, I believe there is a litmus test for the Christian disciple: where we stand in relation to the cross. Our response to the cross is the real test of our spiritual condition.

Our response to the cross is the real test of our spiritual condition.

Are we in front of the cross on our knees in silent worship, or at a distance with our backs turned? Are we left cold, confused, even indifferent by the idea of his death? The verse from Galatians at the beginning of this chapter tells us to be right there on the cross, united with Christ, almost as if we had been stapled together.

After much reflection, Dan said he could see himself worshiping Jesus, but from a distance. During our time of prayer, I sensed that he was moving closer to the cross. Then the penny dropped. Looking at the Christ figure, he said, "I think I should be there with him. I need to die with Christ."

It sounded, on the surface, like an admission of absolute defeat. But here was a man who had decided he had come to the end of himself. And in his words I felt a surge of hope that God could now do anything. This young man's "death" was going to be the release of new life. For anyone who can say those words, "I want to die with Christ," the old really has passed away and the new really has come.

Freedom had come to Dan. He had identified with Christ in his death and was therefore in a position to receive God's version of his future, not his own. It is when we become empty that God begins to fill us. We find that the end of reliance on ourselves is the beginning of dependence on him. As Paul wrote: "I no longer live, but Christ lives in me" (Gal. 2:20).

What Dan experienced was a prayerful revelation that his future was not about "my right to choose" or "my liberty to make what I will of my life," but instead, it was founded on the liberation won for us by God himself. This was surrender, once and for all, to the perfect will of the Father. But I want to suggest that the freedom Dan discovered goes even deeper than that.

Paul wrote in his letter to the church in Galatia that "it is for freedom that Christ has set us free" (5:1). Freedom begins and ends at the cross of Jesus. It was there at Calvary that Christ took on our sins in order that we might be free. Not only was the *penalty* of sin dealt with that day, but the *power* of sin as well. Christ's death and resurrection marked the end of sin's power to control the believer. Therefore, just as sin could not control Jesus, so it is now powerless to control those who put their faith in Christ. Dan no longer need be in thrall to the fears that were crippling him. By pinning them to the cross with Jesus, he was released from their grip.

It is easy to nod in wholehearted agreement, but do we take hold of this freedom in our everyday lives? Or are we still stuck with the same habits and patterns we had before we became Christians? Are we experiencing the promised victory over sin? The joy and contentment that comes in its wake? It's so easy to shrug our shoulders, think nobody's perfect, and plod on, not changing or being set free.

The message of the cross is freedom from sin's penalty—the permanent destruction of a relationship with God—and, in a typically strange and paradoxical way, it presents us with a free ticket to a new way of living. We don't have to keep plodding down the same old paths; we've been offered a new road, with new views and a glorious new horizon.

Freedom in the Workplace

I am often asked what the biggest difference being a Christian makes in the workplace. Paul's words say it all: "The Spirit . . . gives life and has set you free from the law of sin and death" (Rom. 8:2). Often in the harshness of the workplace—the struggle to compete, the demands of performance, the elbowing ambition of colleagues—the workplace comes to reflect death rather than life. Sometimes I can see in the eyes of colleagues a deadness resulting from being worn down by the weariness of life—the demands of travel, the complexity of relationships. They are chasing an illusory freedom that material prosperity is meant to deliver.

Our greatest witness in the world is to draw strength from this new way of living secured through the cross, that we might become witnesses to Christ's restoration of life in all its fullness and stand firm against the dark forces of this evil age (Eph. 6:13), even at the coalface of a demanding work environment.

This new freedom is made plain in the manifesto that defined Christ's ministry:

> "The Spirit of the Lord is on me,
> > because he has anointed me
> > to proclaim good news to the poor.
> He has sent me to proclaim freedom for the prisoners
> > and recovery of sight for the blind,
> to set the oppressed free,
> > to proclaim the year of the Lord's favor."
>
> (Luke 4:18–19)

This is a manifesto of freedom. It means more than just the forgiveness of personal sins. It encompasses the liberation of the whole of humanity from those seemingly uncontrollable forces that appear to dictate our lives. Indeed, according to Peter, Christians are to "live as people who are free, not using [our] freedom as a cover-up for evil, but living as servants of God" (1 Peter 2:16 ESV).

All of us feel under a cloud on some days, or out of control, or as if we're wading through treacle, and life feels full of obstacles. And those are the days when I find it helpful to remind myself that whatever the circumstances and whatever my imperfections,

God is my loving Father, and he has offered me what Paul called "the glorious freedom of God's children" (Rom. 8:21 HCSB). And I choose, in Paul's words, to "press on to take hold of that for which Christ Jesus took hold of me" (Phil. 3:12). On difficult days—and we all have them—I find it helpful to take a break, even if that means getting out of the office for half an hour to take a walk, feel the wind on my face, listen to some worship music, and remember Jesus himself in the garden of Gethsemane, under a cloud and beset by obstacles.

Sometimes, in times of discouragement and despair, as we pray God restores hope in unexpected ways: a verse comes to mind, or a friend calls unexpectedly, or we hear a bird sing, or we watch two old friends greet each other in a café, and we are reminded of the goodness of God and the blessings in our lives. At other times, God seems to highlight some pattern of behavior or ingrained habit that is holding us back. And we know that he is showing us where our darkness comes from. This is how God lovingly convicts us, so that we can live in the light.

Many of us feel trapped by what the Bible calls *strongholds*, an unusual word to describe patterns of behavior and cycles of thought that seem to have us in their grip. We find ourselves obsessed by gaining status or possessions or power; or we feel permanently mean-spirited, insecure, and jealous, unable to rejoice at a friend's success; or we know that we are addicted to drugs or to pornography or even to work.

Even as Christians, we can continue to live bound up by these things, behaving as though Christianity is not good news. If I were to ask you whether or not you are truly free and experiencing true liberation in your walk with Christ, you may be tempted to answer, "Yes, of course." But it's important to pause and search your heart.

Are you constantly battling with anxiety, worry, lust, unforgiveness, anger, a lack of hope, or despondency? Do these patterns of behavior make you feel as though you have no control over your life? If you answered yes to one or all of these questions, then you need to come back to the reality of that freedom purchased for you at the cross.

And, of course, if we are struggling, our struggle can be made worse by knowing that we are falling short. And then the gospel does not feel like the glad tidings of freedom and salvation proclaimed by Jesus, but like a rigid code of dos and don'ts or a list of minimum requirements for the avoidance of punishment. As D. L. Moody famously said: "People have just enough religion to make them miserable."[1]

Don't be fooled by the fact you are not in handcuffs or behind prison bars; you can still be imprisoned in your mind and heart. But do not lose hope. We do not have to strive and strain on our own to achieve this freedom. Paul reassured the Ephesians: "I pray that you may realize how vast are the resources of his Spirit available to you" (3:18 PAR). We can rely on the limitless power of Jesus, if only we have the faith and the courage to ask him.

Whatever we've done, whatever patterns have trapped us, we can choose to accept Christ's pardon. We may have been incarcerated, but Jesus unlocks the prison doors for us with these six simple words: "The truth will set you free" (John 8:32).

One of the many things that compelled me to follow Jesus was the fact that through the victory won at the cross of Calvary I could be set free once and for all. I could be sure, even amid the many challenges and uncertainties in life, that God promised me freedom from the things keeping me captive and in chains.

I read about how every promise in him (Jesus) is both "yes

and amen" (2 Cor. 1:20). Therefore, the prison doors that kept me bound and locked in my sinful habits and thought patterns could be opened and I could walk out, not because of my own bargaining or efforts, but because of the cross of Jesus and the power that lay therein.

I could be changed, transformed, and live a life of power and freedom. John Calvin said, "For so long as we are of the world, we do not belong to Christ."[2] God's desire for each of us is not that we go through life unscathed and without difficulty but that how we live would reflect the position we now have in Christ. We, too, are with Christ in the heavenly places (Eph. 1:3) and have the power of God that is much greater than any present evil or sin trying to lock us back up.

The will of God is not that we escape the world he created—for this is where we have been placed—but rather that sin and evil should have no power over us as we serve God, spreading gospel freedom to all creation, in every sphere of life.

How can we appropriate this new life of freedom—this strange, upside-down kingdom—into our everyday lives?

Here are a few simple steps I have found helpful.

Repentance

Confession is the essential start. Owning up to the fact that we are not fully aligned with Christ's purposes for us starts the process of throwing off everything that holds us back from being effective disciples. We must be specific when we repent. Imagine going to the doctor and simply saying you don't feel very well. It would be very difficult for the doctor to give an effective diagnosis. Sometimes, we find it hard to put into words exactly what we are feeling, but if we start speaking, it helps. At the doctor's we normally start by describing the symptoms, and the doctor helps us work slowly toward the root of the problem. And it is exactly the same with confession. We must name our sin so we can claim God's grace and mercy. This is the first step to finding true freedom.

God wants us to be completely transparent and authentic with him. That includes confessing our sins, which he knows about anyway. He's not looking for perfection. He's looking for complete honesty, vulnerability, and sincerity. When I read the Gospel accounts, I see that Jesus reserved his harshest words for those who hid behind a curtain of righteousness based upon their own apparently virtuous behavior, and that he denounced the insincerity and hypocrisy of the Pharisees.

David wrote Psalm 51 after he committed adultery with Bathsheba, and we see him begging God for mercy, love, and compassion in the face of his wrongdoing: "Against you . . . have I sinned and done what is evil in your sight" (v. 4). And, "You desire truth in the inward parts" (v. 6 NKJV). That's it—truth with ourselves and truth with God as we ask him to create in us "a pure heart" (v. 10). God doesn't expect perfection, but he does ask us to repent with honesty. You can either pretend to be perfect or you can repent. In my experience, it's one or the other. You can't do both.

And we need to do this regularly, perhaps in the evening as we reflect on our day and identify the ways in which we have fallen short of living in a good relationship with God and with others.

> **You can either pretend to be perfect or you can repent. In my experience, it's one or the other. You can't do both.**

"If we confess our sins, he is faithful and just to forgive us our sins, and to cleanse us from all unrighteousness" (1 John 1:9 KJV).

At Calvary's cross Jesus broke the chains, broke the curse, and broke the code of sin that was written into our DNA from the fall of Adam and Eve. When we confess to God, he doesn't just edit out our sins, but he edits in our righteousness. When humanity repents, God does not try to take something away as much as he tries to give something back. That something has been placed into every human being on earth—it is the image of God.

Surrender

If there is to be a new start in life, it means getting rid of the old life. The Spirit must have free rein throughout our lives without any compartmentalizing or qualifying what he may do or where he may go. It is what the preacher and pastor Samuel Chadwick euphorically declared as being the key to unlocking heaven's blessing:

> Things not surrendered, indulgences retained against light, possessions held or selfish ends—these must all be surrendered to the supreme authority of Christ. For until he is exalted, crowned, glorified, there can be no Pentecost.[3]

Acceptance of Grace

After confession and surrender, there is a need to choose to grasp and accept the power of grace. Grace is the foundation upon which the whole gospel of freedom in Christ is built. If we have no understanding of this grace that delivers us from the power of sin, we will be a bound church, feebly trying to break the chains and strongholds in our own strength.

True deliverance and freedom are birthed when the gospel is drawn into our lives and compels us to embrace it in its fullness. It is birthed when people are set free—not just from the fact of guilt and their shame, but also from the power of evil and the toxic pollution of sin. True freedom leads to a new confidence, courage, and boldness. And boldness before the throne of grace leads to boldness and being fearless before people.

In Acts chapter 5 we see the apostles appearing before the Sanhedrin to be questioned by the high priest, who admonishes them, saying, "We gave you strict orders not to teach in this name . . . yet you have filled Jerusalem with your teaching and are determined to make us guilty of this man's blood" (v. 28). And now we see that true freedom in Christ leads to boldness. "Peter and the other apostles replied: 'We must obey God rather than human beings!'" (v. 29).

When truly set free, the people of God become extraordinary forces for good in the world. Transformed hearts, set free from the past, are a force to be reckoned with. It happens to us as individuals in our one-on-one relationship with God, and it happens corporately, as a church, the body of Christ.

That is why a book written on the cross is not a mournful tale, but a triumphant one. Yes, we experience a mix of emotions as we contemplate the suffering of the Son of God, but we know that the cry Jesus gave—"It is finished"—was not the cry of the vanquished but the cry of a victor. These words were filled with faith that, in spite of everything, the favor

When truly set free, the people of God become extraordinary forces for good in the world.

of God still rested upon him and the purposes of God could not and would not be thwarted. It was a cry that seemed to mark an ending, but in fact heralded a new beginning. And when we "die to Christ," we begin anew.

As Leslie Newbiggin wrote:

> The event of the resurrection, the empty tomb and the risen Lord breaks every mold that would imprison God in the rationalism of a fallen world. But it is the starting point of a new kind of rationality, for the possibility of living hopefully in a world without hope, for the perpetual praise of God who not only creates order out of chaos but also breaks through fixed orders to create ever-new situations of surprise and joy.[4]

And because we cannot imprison God in the rationalism of a fallen world, I entitled this book *Strange Kingdom*. And it is a strange kingdom wherein I am crucified with Christ and thus made free. At a rational level it is inconceivable, incomprehensible even. And yet, curiously, in the dimension that the Bible calls deep unto deep, it resonates.

I remember walking along a London street when I was a young banker. I passed the Bank of England, and, looking up, I saw a towering edifice of solidity and security. It was, to me at that time, a symbol of trust. But at that moment I stopped on the pavement, and I prayed that God would set me free from all that it represented—the dominance of economics in every aspect of life. There was no particular thunderbolt moment and no immediate feeling of release, but it was certainly the beginning of a process of getting free from the unhealthy hold the financial world had over me. On that street I had to "die" to that part of me, surrender it to

God. And Paul's statement to the Galatians leapt into my heart: "I have died with Christ. Yet I live" (2:20 PAR).

This passage may be well-known and the underlying theology commonplace at the intellectual level. Yet, when it hits you personally as an existential truth, it's rather disorientating. And, certainly, decidedly odd! I have died, yet I am not dead—I am alive. Except now "I live by faith in the Son of God, who loved me and gave himself for me" (v. 20).

And there on that street in London, I was struck by the thought that one day even the Bank of England, both the physical building and the venerable institution, will crumble. But faith placed in Jesus Christ is secure forever because he will never change and never die. The cross has secured for us the only foundation our lives will ever need. The cross is the bridge over which we walk into freedom. The apparent weakness of Jesus lifted up onto a cross by evil men has unleashed the power of God. We remain weak and frail human beings. But when we are weak, we are strong because of the love and power of God.

The kingdom of God is open to all: the rich and the poor; the educated and the uneducated; those who are strong and those who are weak. We are, each one of us, members of this fellowship: purchased by the blood of Christ, brought together by the working of the Holy Spirit, and protected by the victory Jesus won on the cross, which made us inheritors of this new kingdom.

Ministry to Each Other

Sometimes we need to allow the Holy Spirit to minister this freedom to us. Not every stronghold can be broken by ourselves. One of the greatest contributions of successive leaders at my home church, HTB in London, is to emphasize in every service the importance of ministry to each other. By ministry, I mean the creation of a safe space within a setting of worship for people to come forward and be prayed for, to be released from those things that hold them captive and the patterns of behavior that destroy freedom. It has been a huge privilege both to pray and be prayed for in these services.

Christ knows the entire stories of your life and my life, and he wants to set us free from the hurts of the past to enable us to live in hope for the future. The freedom that Christ alone can bring is so much more than the ability to come to terms with our past. Psychiatrists, psychologists, and cognitive therapists can help us do that, and we thank God for their expertise. But Jesus Christ can actually liberate us from our past, so that it no longer has a hold on us.

> **Christ knows the entire stories of your life and my life, and he wants to set us free from the hurts of the past to enable us to live in hope for the future.**

In Ian McEwan's novel *Atonement*—and in Joe Wright's film based on the book—an acclaimed novelist, coming to the end of her life, tries to put right the terrible consequences of her actions as a child by creating a work of fiction in which the people whose lives she destroyed are offered a happy ending. She hoped to find relief and atonement in the act of rewriting the story, but the exercise proved unsatisfactory—useless, in fact. Obviously, her fiction couldn't resurrect the people whose lives she had destroyed, and neither could it bring her peace. Interestingly, the fictional happy ending also seemed insufficient for film audiences, who left cinemas in tears. We are creatures and not gods, and however gifted we are, we cannot rewrite our pasts or write our futures. But thank God we don't have to because Jesus has already done it for us.

I heard a story a few years ago about a team of investigators being urgently dispatched to the sewers of London. They discovered a mass of congealed cooking fat combined with thousands of diapers, fifteen stone in weight and the size of a double-decker bus. It was so huge, in fact, that it caused the entire system of the city's drains to collapse. This is a good picture of what hidden sin does to us.

If we think that chucking another diaper down the toilet won't make any difference, or sloshing more cooking fat down the drain will be harmless, we are sorely mistaken. This stuff doesn't disappear. It goes somewhere, and it congeals and solidifies. The more we sin, the more it builds up, and at some point, the whole thing collapses.

In London all traffic was diverted, and a huge operation began. Workers armed with power hoses spent three weeks breaking down the mass. And finally they dislodged it. It is the Holy Spirit who has the power to sweep clean the garbage in the sewers of our minds, to jettison all that weighs us down and blocks us up, and, in doing so, eliminate the considerable unnecessary suffering in our lives that is not born of God.

The Hillsong worship group Young and Free capture this brilliantly in Aodhan King's song "This Is Living," in which black and white turn to color and life is a gift to be lived to death. And there it is—living is dying and dying is living—it's the paradox with which we began. The song has had a huge global reach precisely because it affirms this great truth of the cross: that there is a new and uniquely liberating way of living.

> **The power of the Spirit is unleashed with astonishing force through the apparent folly of the cross.**

The power of the Spirit flows from the cross, frees us from the chains of sin and death, unlocks our prison doors, and leads us to feast at the Master's table. The power of the Spirit is unleashed with astonishing force through the apparent folly of the cross.

The prayer that rises from my heart is this: may you come to know for the first time or in a new way, in surpassing and abundant measure, the freedom that is yours in the powerful love of Jesus Christ crucified.

A Time to Meditate

Music

- "This Is Living," Aodhan King, Young and Free
- *Adagio, String Quintet in C Major*, Franz Schubert

Reflect

- Sometimes we feel stuck—helpless before patterns of behavior and ingrained habits that shame us and stunt us. Whatever we've done and wherever we're stuck, God is our deliverer. If you feel locked in a dark place, imagine Jesus coming and opening the padlock with six words: "The truth will set you free." You can respond by saying, "I receive your freedom. I am set free."

- There are only two choices after all: to pretend to be perfect or to repent with honesty. But we can't do both. And God knows all about us anyway! There are harsh words for the hypocrites and the insincere but only love for the sincerely sorry. Being sincerely sorry sets us free. And it's the truest thing we could ever do.
- Now we're free. Take that in—we are *free*. And in that freedom we can grasp the power of his grace and live in hope for the future.

Prayer

Lord, thank you that it is for freedom that Christ has set us free. As we walk in grace we have not earned, help us to show the power of your love to others that they, too, might be set free. We receive your freedom, and we commit to use it to serve you and serve each other to your glory, by the power of your Spirit, amen.

SEVEN

FORLORN

At the place where Jesus was crucified, there was a garden, and in the garden a new tomb, in which no one had ever been laid. Because it was the Jewish day of Preparation and since the tomb was nearby, they laid Jesus there. Early on the first day of the week, while it was still dark, Mary Magdalene went to the tomb and saw that the stone had been removed from the entrance.

—John 19:41—20:1

THE BODY OF CHRIST IS FORLORN—AS SILENT AS THE
tombstone that guards it. Jesus spoke before the high priest and
religious leaders on Friday. He will liberate humanity of sin and
death on Sunday. But on Saturday he along with the whole earth
is shrouded in complete and utter silence. The tomb is a waiting
room, and those who wait pace up and down, hoping for some
news, a sign, a symbol of hope. Little do they know that under-
neath the story of death, darkness, and despair is a hidden story
of God's resurrection power and glory. In the midst of the deathly
silence of Saturday, is it possible that something glorious could be
waiting to be birthed?

Friday had been so full of activity:

> From noon until three in the afternoon darkness came over all
> the land. . . . And when Jesus had cried out again in a loud voice,
> he gave up his spirit. At that moment the curtain of the temple
> was torn in two from top to bottom. The earth shook, the rocks
> split and the tombs broke open. The bodies of many holy people
> who had died were raised to life. (Matt 27:45, 50–52)

On Friday, God blocked the sun, Jesus offered himself as the
perfect sacrifice, God tore the temple curtain, opened tombs, and
raised the dead. But on Saturday, God, too, was silent.

Why is it that Easter weekend services tend to pass over the
solemn silence of Saturday? The crucifixion and resurrection

command, dictate, and own our thoughts. But what about Saturday? The supreme drama of the passion narrative tells of three days that form the fulcrum and turning point of all human history. Yet the center of this drama itself is a waiting room. It seems all the action and emotion belong to two days only: hopelessness and joy, evil and good, defeat and ultimate victory, the end of one era and the beginning of another, evenly balanced in stark contrast between what the Roman soldiers did to Jesus on Good Friday and what God did for him on Sunday.

None of the Gospel writers convey or take the time to show any interest in the waiting room that sits between the two great moments in human history—except for Matthew, who describes that on the next day the religious leaders gathered together before Pilate on the morning of the day of preparation, urgently asking to take away the body, as special measures to make certain that nothing would happen at the tomb (Matt. 27:62). Otherwise, between Jesus' death and resurrection, there is a period of silence, a lifeless void. There is only a time of waiting in which nothing speaks and nothing of importance occurs and of which there is little to be shown or said.

For much of Christian history, the day has found little place in the Easter story, except the stripping of the altars in Catholic traditions—and it might be thought a bizarre and irrelevant starting point for meditation. The second day appears to be a barren land, an anonymous waiting period in the gospel narrative. A day that can boast no identity for itself, no fixed season, and can claim no true meaning, reflecting only the experiences it can borrow and remember from what comes before and after.

But does this silent Saturday—the state between the cross and resurrection—have a significant meaning, a distinct revelation, that brings to light the atrocities of Friday and the new birth of Sunday? Might not the place between Calvary's cross and the garden tomb be the best of all starting places from which to meditate upon what happened at Golgotha, in the tomb, and in the waiting room of in between? The in-between God is a reality as much as the intervening God of Friday and Sunday. The halfway point, at the heart of the unfolding mystery, might itself provide an excellent perspective from which to observe the narrative and its true meaning. Alan Lewis described that "day between the days" as one that "speaks solely neither of the cross nor of the resurrection, but simultaneiously remembers the one and awaits the other, and guarantees that neither will be heard, or thought about, or lived, without the other."[1]

I am sure many of us can relate to this state of being. I know of numerous seasons in my own life when I am caught in this tension of waiting, as one stage of my life ends and I wait for the next cycle to be birthed and for my own creative impulses, hopes, and desires to be breathed to life. There is a sense of expectation and anticipation of what will come, but also a sadness at what has been lost and perhaps fear that the pause will last longer than I can bear.

Paul wrote, "I delivered to you as of first importance what I also received: that Christ died for our sins in accordance with the Scriptures, that he was buried, that he was raised on the third day in accordance with the Scriptures" (1 Cor. 15:3–4 ESV). He was buried. No more is said. Jesus is truly dead among the dead, cut off from the living, gone from this world into eternal silence. And we grieve for what has been lost. To skip past the silence of Saturday to the victory that Sunday brings is to deny the difficult reality of Jesus' death and the grief of the first believers.

Saturday is a day that forces us to reflect and meditate at

the place of the tomb and to try and understand how it could be possible that Jesus, God's own Son, united from the beginning of time, lay motionless, lifeless, within the sealed tomb. It is the day between the struggle and the solution, the question and the answer, the offered prayer and the answer thereof. Why the pause? Why does God remain silent in the midst of our struggles when he knows the answers? Where is God when we find ourselves sitting in the silent tomb of Saturday?

Where is God when we find ourselves sitting in the silent tomb of Saturday?

We wait for a word from God to be spoken into our suffering: the pain of the rejection of a dear friend, the death of a loved one, the agony of unemployment and no apparent prospects, the heartbreak of a troubled marriage. We wait desperately to hear a word of meaning, of hope and consolation. Very often there is nothing but silence. And to us in this noisy, restless, instant-fix world that is forever on the move, silence is terrifying and waiting is unbearable. Why did Jesus not rise from the grave on Friday evening? Why the three days of waiting? Why the need for silence? What was the point of it? Is there perhaps something profound for his followers to learn from the silence?

Saturday is about waiting with uncertainty, about muddling through, even when the future isn't clear. But it is also the time when the Holy Spirit is "hovering," as he was at the beginning of time, before the creation of the world—"brooding," as some translations call it. If we can dare to enter the silence and stay with that silence, we, too, are taken back to the very beginning of creation, to the formless, empty void described in the book of Genesis.

And, in that apparent nothingness, once again we come face-to-face with the Creator who is quite at home in voids, working gently and lovingly to create new life—indeed, risen life! Imagine a frozen river in the back garden of our lives, apparently dead. No matter how dark and still the river looks or how frozen it becomes, in Christ there is always the power of resurrected life flowing beneath the depths.

We sit and wait, trying our best to be patient, unsure of what will unfold, as we desperately hope and pray for a better tomorrow. Saturday is the day that Jesus was locked in a tomb, heaven fell silent, and the disciples waited in confusion. When a person exhausts all manner of certainty and the existing data leaves us more confused, faith is what an individual must hold on to, as he tries to discern God's will and simply believe what God has previously said.

> No matter how dark and still the river looks or how frozen it becomes, in Christ there is always the power of resurrected life flowing beneath the depths.

From my own experiences, I have found the silence of Saturday to be a time when I have to trust God's in control and trust his rule and reign, even if my expectations haven't been met and I am filled with disappointment. It is a helpless state, in which we cling to a childlike faith that our human knowledge can't conceive. At times like this, we don't need more knowledge. Oftentimes our level of obedience and trust cannot keep up with the level of revelation we have already received. In these moments of suffering and pain, we must trust God and accept his will, even when it seems contrary to our own.

Enduring the Silence

When I think of the forlorn Saturday experience, I think of the Old Testament character Job. As the curtains open we enter a divine conversation between God and Satan. In the beginning of this story everything is as we think it should be, everything is okay. But trouble is coming to Uz, trouble is coming to Job. Uz is the place where bad things happen to good people; Uz is the place where suffering comes but it comes without warning and explanation and God seems absent. Uz is the land of silence.

The Devil strikes up an audience with God and questions him. He uses Job as a case study and asks God to let him attack every aspect of Job's life to prove Job will only worship God when he feels blessed. Will Job worship in the silence? Will Job worship God amid the loss, the suffering, and despair? Is Job devoted to God because of the blessings he accumulates, or will he sit and curse God as scabs cover him from his head down to the soles of his feet?

Job lost more than most of us will lose in a lifetime. He lost his family, his health, and his livelihood, but he didn't lose his trust in God. As Job grieved, he held on to God in faith and love and goodness. When it didn't seem to pay off in the moment, Job remained faithful. When the only voices he heard were the poor theodicies put forward by his friends to explain his suffering, Job sat there, long after they'd left him, in the silence, continuing to trust God. Little did Job realize something cosmic and vast and eternal was at stake in his life. Job acknowledged the pain of his loss, but it awakened the steadfast foundation that can only come from being rooted in God.

Job is just one example of the many heroes of the faith who had to live through the silence of Saturday.

I think of Dr. Martin Luther King Jr., the prominent civil rights leader in the twentieth century. He was a Baptist minister and a devoted follower of Christ. Dr. King played a significant role in the social justice movement. In December 1955, a young woman named Rosa Parks was arrested for refusing to give up her seat on a bus to a white man. Local pastors in the area rallied together the black community for a citywide movement, called the Montgomery Improvement Association,[2] and elected King as president. He lived under constant pain and hardship. On one occasion his home was bombed, he was regularly threatened with violence, and at a book signing he was stabbed in the chest. Yet still he was committed to seeing the end of prejudice and racism in America.

Dr. King had what is often referred to as a holy discontent that inspired him to wake up every day and attempt to bring the necessary changes to America. This inspired his famous speech "I Have a Dream." Despite knowing he might not see the day of liberation in his own lifetime, he was committed to suffering and experiencing the struggle for a greater cause.

We can so often focus on the benefits of what being a Christian entails. We recognize that we are redeemed, restored, and renewed and fail to see that a key part of the Christian walk is to suffer, often without explanation. It can be a time when hopelessness seems to have the last laugh and with the psalmist we cry, "How long, LORD? Will you forget me forever? How long will you hide your face from me?" (Ps. 13:1).

Perhaps we can relate to the two disciples as they walked the seven-mile stretch on the road to Emmaus. They had Jesus in their presence but failed to recognize him because they were so disappointed about what they perceived as unfulfilled. And can we blame them? They witnessed their friend and Savior being tortured at the hands of the Roman soldiers. They experienced the trauma of seeing their best friend die a sinner's death. And as they walked down this road, away from Jerusalem, the place they were asked to stay and wait, they were blinded by pain and despair.

The disciples on the road to Emmaus are a picture of the hopelessness we often feel in the silence of Saturday, a time when Sunday seems so far off, and Friday is at the forefront of our minds. In the original language in which this passage was written, Luke describes the two disciples not just talking with each other about everything that had happened (24:14) but literally talking over each other, shouting, trying to make sense of things and piece together exactly what had happened during the previous week.

On Saturday God is present but appears to be absent. It is easy for us to look at Easter Saturday and the road to Emmaus through the lens of what we know about the events of Sunday. As we know, Jesus has resurrected and triumphed over sin, its power, and the grave. In the same way, I often watch the great soccer matches from the past that I've seen hundreds of times, knowing exactly who scores when and what the final result will be. The first time I watched the game, it was full of tension and drama. But the highlights don't give me the same experience. I always know the ending!

We don't have to navigate our way through that first Saturday and the silence that enveloped the disciples the way they did. We know the final score, we know who wins! We know death is defeated! It takes a lot of the tension out of the "in-between space" and gives us a sense of peace knowing what happened and how it unfolded. Yet life in real time is rarely experienced in that way. When we don't know how the situation will be resolved or whether the relationship will be restored, in the midst of our uncertainty, it can be hard to maintain confidence in God's sovereignty.

In its silence, Saturday is the longest day of all. Seconds would have felt like hours, minutes like days, the agony of sitting in the waiting room. Jesus was gone, death had apparently swallowed him up without a fight. What we know now, the early disciples did not know. Every year Christians call the Friday of Easter week "good" because they know the final score. But to those early Christians, living in the tension, lingering in the silence of Saturday as they grieved the loss of their friend would have been agony.

We have the propensity and proclivity to skip over Friday, linger by the tomb on Saturday, and then jump from the tomb on Saturday. Instead of sitting in the silence, we jump to the resurrection. Theologian Hans Urs von Balthasar wrote: "We must guard against that theological busyness and religious impatience which insist on anticipating the moment of fruiting the eternal redemption through the temporal passion—on dragging forward that moment from Easter to Holy Saturday."[3] When we find ourselves suffering on Friday and sitting in the waiting room of silent Saturday, we must not be too ferocious in our activity to fall on our knees and meditate on the barred tomb in that moment.

As we wait in the cold darkness of the tomb, the only difficulty is that we know the ending. Those original disciples—heartbroken and despairing after watching their Lord hang helplessly on the cross—didn't know what Sunday would bring, notwithstanding Jesus' explanation that he would rebuild the temple in three days and the prophetic literature of Israel pointing to the vindication of the Suffering Servant. To the disciples, Saturday seemed utterly final. And even when we get to Sunday, we must remember that this isn't the end of the journey. Saturday will come again. It always does.

Personally, I have found this time of waiting the hardest of all spiritual disciplines. Leaving the certainties of one phase of

I know of no mature disciple of Christ who has not experienced the deep frustration of waiting for God to act.

my life and trying to embrace the waiting is wretched. It all seems so pointless. Why wait when we can be getting on with life? But I know of no mature disciple of Christ who has not experienced the deep frustration of waiting for God to act.

When heaven seems to be as brass and there is no sign of life, waiting to hear what God is calling us to next can be such a trying time. God, apparently, is not around to show us the next steps to the abundant life we long for. Like Habakkuk we cry, "How long, LORD, must I call for help, but you do not listen?" (Hab. 1:2). But let us take heart from the verse that follows later: "Though it linger, wait for it; it will certainly come and will not delay" (2:3).

Silent but Not Absent

God may be silent, but he is not absent. He knows and he cares. Even in the deafening silence of that Saturday tomb, we can still, like Mary Magdalene, call him our Lord.

God may be silent, but he is not absent.

Wherever you turn in the Bible, you will find yourself in good company if you are experiencing the silent, empty void of Saturday. Look at the dream boy Joseph, thrust into a waiting room in the bowels of an Egyptian prison. He was not idle though. He took the opportunity to exercise his gift of prophecy, which two years later resulted in his release from prison and his promotion to prime minister of Egypt.

I am always amazed that the Gospels speak very little of the disciples' response on Saturday to Jesus' death. But they do say that before the sun had set on that first Good Friday, Joseph of Arimathea came to the religious authorities and asked for Jesus' body, that it might be buried, and his friend could rest in peace. "Joseph of Arimathea asked Pilate for the body of Jesus. Now Joseph was a disciple of Jesus. . . . he came and took the body away" (John 19:38). It's a verse I've passed over time and time again.

John wrote that after the crowds had disappeared and the groans of those being executed fell mute and ceased, Joseph made the short journey to pick up Jesus' broken, dead body as the silence of Saturday drew near. I can picture the scene in my mind: Joseph carefully and tenderly carrying Jesus' body from the cross, which a few hours earlier was being laughed at and mocked, as he suffocated in public for all to see. I can imagine the nail marks, the stains of blood, around Jesus' hands and feet. It wasn't just the weight of Jesus' body that would have burdened Joseph of Arimathea; it would have been the memories of what had occurred a few hours earlier, imaging over and over again the devastating scenes that had unfolded before his very eyes at the foot of Calvary's hill. The despair and grief must have been unbearable, hopeless and confused, all expectation of life now gone.

Years earlier, we presume, Joseph had left behind his life of predictability and safety to follow an unknown Master. He was clearly a man of influence and affluence—a member of the council who had pressed for the death of Jesus. But he was a man of conscience and did not go with the majority decision.

He was doing the right thing because it was the right thing to do. But now Joseph held his best friend, and the future hope of his people, dead in his arms. This was not part of the plan. It wasn't meant to end this way. He had held so tightly to the small seed of hope that Jesus really was who he said he was, but he felt like a fool. He must have thought he was delusional to believe that this man, this figure, this rabbi could be the coming Messiah. What a pointless pursuit. What a waste of three years. But—and this is the key to this often-overlooked passage—Joseph showed up in the midst of his grief that night, determined, despite the despondence of what looked like the finality and hopelessness of the event, to carry the weight of Jesus' dead body and hold it in his no doubt shaking arms.

Joseph voluntarily asked for Jesus' body. It wasn't forced upon him; he didn't draw the short straw. He experienced this burden due to his own volition and choice. Was it that he wanted to honor Jesus, even in his death? To follow him, even to the point of his finality? I believe that this is such an important and profound point to dwell on. When we sign up to a life of following Jesus, we have to accept that we will experience the glory of the resurrection as well the burden of the crucifixion. But for all of us there are Saturdays when all we have is the weight and the burden of taking the body of Christ onto our own frames. Like Joseph of Arimathea, we carry the dead weight of Christ. In his case, it was literal, but, in our case, we carry the weight within our very beings.

When we sign up to a life of following Jesus, we have to accept that we will experience the glory of the resurrection as well as the burden of the crucifixion.

Dietrich Bonhoeffer, who you will remember inspired me with the title of this book, carried the weight of Christ throughout his life, even to his death. While the despotic power of Hitler raged around him in Nazi

Germany, he appropriated the cause of Christ and held up high a torch of goodness and sacrifice in the dark world that surrounded him. The burden of Christ can be heavy and can be harsh. Those facing persecution for their faith today live in constant uncertainty, their lives under threat every day. Others live in circumstances of extreme suffering for prolonged periods, even their whole lives.

But for others of us, our burdens are not so extreme, though still painful. We perhaps bear the silence of God at times of stress in our lives and relationships. We long to hear God's voice and see his light, but his absence feels like a lifeless weight bearing down on our souls in the shadows. But this, it seems, is part of the deal. Joseph of Arimathea carried the corpse of Christ, and bore the accompanying silence, even though he did not know that Resurrection Sunday was around the corner.

There is a painting illustrating the narrative poem called "Footprints," which you may be familiar with. Walking down the beach, a man talks to God as he remembers the different stages of his life. The man's life journey is represented by footprints in the sand. Usually there are two sets of prints: one belonging to him and one belonging to God. He notices, however, that during the troubled periods of his life, only one set of footprints is evident in the sand. The man asks God where he was during those difficult times. Why, at the times when he needed him most, was there only one set of footprints in the sand? And God replies that those were the times that God carried him.

The poem is beautiful. Yet for me it misses something crucial about Christian faith. God does carry us. I believe that whole-heartedly. But sometimes our walk of faith is so challenging that it feels that we are carrying Jesus, that we are suffering with him.

One of the Old Testament words for *glory* is the Hebrew word *kabod*, which means weightiness. We carry Christ in our hearts, and sometimes the weight of this burden is so substantial that we are left forlorn, downcast, and hopeless. This is the "in-between" Saturday part of our faith. Like Job and Joseph of Arimathea who have gone before, we must acknowledge that faith isn't just Good Friday and Easter Sunday, faith is the silence of Saturday too. In his book *A Glorious Dark*, Dr. A. J. Swoboda wrote, "So much is sitting in that tomb with the soon-to-be resurrected Lord. It is so dark. So cold. So scary. The silence is deafening. But there is hope in there."[4] "Immanuel, God with us" is as much true in the darkness of the tomb as it is when the sun rises and the stone is rolled away.

Jesus entered his tomb alone and forlorn, but he didn't stay there. Jesus welcomes us into the hope that Sunday *is* coming, that he *is* coming. And that changes everything.

A Time to Meditate

Music

- "Take Courage," Bethel Music, Kristene DiMarco
- "Lux Aeterna," Edward Elgar

Reflect

- Perhaps life feels messy. I encourage you to join Joseph of Arimathea as he enters a messy bit of Jesus' story.

Perhaps nothing has turned out as you hoped. It was the same for Joseph. Perhaps you can't see how it all ends. It was the same for Joseph. As you sit with him, forlorn by the tomb, ask God for patience and peace in the waiting and the fearing and the not-knowing.

- Now, ask the Creator Spirit to come and breathe life and hope into your place of loss, fear, and unknowing. As you repeat, "Come, Holy Spirit," it may help you to imagine the frozen surface of the river and to ask God to come and thaw your fears and to release in his time the new life beneath.

- Let your whirring mind become quiet and God's love for you become louder. Let the cold of fear and stress give way to the warmth of God's presence. Join the disciples on the road to Emmaus, who suddenly saw that Jesus was right beside them. He's right beside you too. The night is ending, and the new dawn will come.

Prayer

Lord, on my silent Saturdays, today or whenever they come, I choose not to flinch. I choose to say with Mary Magdalene that you are still my Lord. And I trust that after every Saturday comes Sunday, after the crucifixion is resurrection, and after death is life. Come, Lord Jesus, amen.

EIGHT

FULFILLED

He said to them, "This is what I told you while I was still with you: Everything must be fulfilled that is written about me in the Law of Moses, the Prophets and the Psalms." Then he opened their minds so they could understand the Scriptures. He told them, "This is what is written: The Messiah will suffer and rise from the dead on the third day, and repentance for the forgiveness of sins will be preached in his name to all nations, beginning at Jerusalem. You are witnesses of these things. I am going to send you what my Father has promised; but stay in the city until you have been clothed with power from on high."

—Luke 24:44–49

AT THE CROSS, THE DECISIVE EVENT IN HUMAN HIS-
tory has taken place. It is the pivotal point of the greatest reversal
ever known: the place where sin, death, and the powers of this
world were defeated, once and for all. There is nothing more central to the Christian life than this. But we can't stop here. The
cross of Jesus doesn't only eliminate the problems of sin and death,
nor does it only answer humanity's longing for God; it also marks
the prophetic fulfillment of the countdown to a brand-new community. This is a community that truly knows the power of joy.
Not the downcast, grim, killjoy Christian of popular thought; it is
the opposite. This is a community empowered like no other then
or since to change the world in which we live by being changed
ourselves.

All Christians now have a mandate to fulfill and the power to
achieve it. And to miss this would be to form an anemic picture
of what was achieved at the cross. Through the cross we enter day
one of a new era in history. The inauguration of a new dawn is
followed and fulfilled by the resurrection and the giving of the
Spirit at Pentecost. Taken together, these three events—the cross,
the resurrection, and the giving of the Holy Spirit—initiate and
empower our agenda for change in the world.

The prophecy of the Old Testament has been fulfilled, as is
seen in the verse from Luke's Gospel above, and its fulfillment
leads to our fulfillment as purposeful human beings, released into
the world by God. We are to be *in* the world, changing it to be

Taken together, these three events—the cross, the resurrection, and the giving of the Holy Spirit—initiate and empower our agenda for change in the world.

more aligned with the message of the good news of Jesus. But we are not *of* it. We can see into both the kingdom of this world and the kingdom of our Lord and King. This is the beauty of the strange kingdom that Jesus has established through his life, death, and resurrection.

For the cross to be a victory, its power must give us the strength to face the demands and pressures of life's battles and to understand at a deeper level the nature of those battles. The battle Jesus faced wasn't a game of power and prestige in the traditional, orthodox, first-century sense, personified and established by Roman rule and reign. Rather, it was a battle that we can only understand in light of seeing his death as the start of a new age.

Every sermon he preached, every person he touched, every demon he expelled, and every person he fed formed part of the continuous sacrifice of himself to reconnect us to our Father and to bring in the new kingdom—a kingdom not of power and prestige according to the world's terms, but of sacrifice and service according to God's terms. Jesus came to bring the kingdom of God to earth, to serve and not to be served, and "to give his life as a ransom for many" (Mark 10:45).

The cross of Jesus, therefore, becomes the fullest expression of the love of God for us. Those two words *for us* are used again and again in the New Testament. "God made him who had no sin to be sin *for us*, so that in him we might become the righteousness of God" (2 Cor. 5:21, emphasis added).

This was not a solo act. Jesus didn't die for himself. He died not as an example of self-sacrifice or as a failed zealot or as an act of suicide for a cause, but *for us*. He did not die for some new religious philosophy or to make a point; he died *for us*. These two short words have such extraordinary power, defining in stunning brevity the whole meaning of the cross. No two words have shaped the history of humankind more than they have. In this ultimate act of sacrifice, Christ died to enable us to taste true freedom. And within *us* is contained every generation of humankind—past, present, and future—all of whom are offered liberation by the death of Christ.

At its core, his love put others—all others—ahead of himself. "God so loved the world that he gave his one and only Son, that whoever believes in him shall not perish but have eternal life" (John 3:16). Eternal life and eternal love. He will never let us die again. Nor can we ever be unloved again. But "for us" is precisely that. It's not for me alone. It's both personal and communal. Through his death, he formed a new community and opened up a new way of living. This is not just an individual journey. That he died "for me" is trenchantly true, but of greater significance is that he died "for us" so that the living church might become a community of beneficiaries of his love. The cross is about love, but it is also supremely about life—the new life that we can enjoy together in Jesus Christ.

> **Jesus did not die for some new religious philosophy or to make a point; he died *for us*.**

The Longing for Love

The greatest mistake we make is to spiritualize the cross of Christ and treat his death as relevant only for contemplative or religious purposes. We need to restore the cross of Christ to the center of our day-to-day lives, not as some morbid reflection of our eventual mortality, but as a way of understanding that this unsurpassed act of love creates the very foundation for our lives together in our communities, churches, cities, and countries.

The unnerving fact of our culture is that, although the desire for love is overwhelmingly strong and strengthening by the day, love as it is currently understood is not working. At every level of society, we see the breakdown of relationships, not only in divorce and separation, but also in a myriad of other ways: in the coarsening of language in everyday conversation and in the ubiquitous identification of pornography with love.

Millions of people tuned in for the finale of *Love Island*, the UK reality dating show in which the encounters of young men and women in search of love were filmed. The media attention to the on-set sexual activities of the participants was almost always couched in the language of seeking love, but essentially this was just permissible porn for a prime-time audience. Few, if any, of these relationships have outlived the series. And yet, at the same time, everyone longs for love, for the real thing. I have never come across a person who is so self-contained as not to want to love and be loved.

The desire to form and enjoy loving relationships is implanted deep in the heart of humanity, but the truth is that the world around us produces a version of love that simply isn't satisfying. What Proverbs tells us is undoubtedly true: "What a person desires is unfailing love" (19:22). This is true of every person, every generation, and every culture in every age of history—people long to find authentic and true love. For that reason, love is the subject matter of 80 percent of the new songs that are written by contemporary songwriters—mostly about the yearning for love, the pain of rejection, and the struggle for fulfillment.

The cross speaks into this longing and goes the extra mile in answering our lifelong questions about love. The cross was an act of sacrifice in which Christ showed his love for us by giving his own life. But it is the fulfillment of the self—and not sacrifice—that is the way of our age. Today love tends to be conditional, self-interested, and only "for as long as it lasts," as opposed to Christ's love that is unconditional, sacrificial, and continual in every scenario and circumstance.

The cross opened up a new way of living inspired by love, and from it a new plan for humanity emerged. As Christ fulfilled his calling to liberate us for a new life of purpose and direction, so we are enabled to know our why, to find our purpose in the world, and to execute in our day-to-day living what he initiated on the cross. We are now able to help shape the world around us in a new hope-filled and love-directed way, rather than be shaped by uncontrollable forces trying to convince us to find our way alone, feeding the ever-hungry demands of the self.

Darkness is no longer the dominant force in the world, but through Jesus' death, light has come to bring radical change to our lives, that we might bring radical change to the world around us. The "same old, same old" way of living no longer applies. All is made new in this post-cross world. In his death a new regime was birthed. And this regime, unlike any other, has lived for thousands of years and will never end. It's the regime founded on hope for the future and power for living now.

I am often asked whether being a Christian makes me a better banker than my colleagues. "No," I tend to reply, "not a better banker, but a better Ken." But that is a deficient answer. Because of what Christ did on the cross, I have a new calling. I am a new Ken, not just a better Ken. I am now an agent for change in the world, empowered to bring light into dark corners because the cross has inaugurated a new society free from the powerful grip of greed and self-interest.

The cross is the decisive victory of God's way in the world, and the resurrection is the empowering victory—the first sign of this new era. We should, therefore, never regard the cross simply as a sin-exchange mechanism that has personal benefits in terms of the freedom we can enjoy as a result. On the contrary, what excites and motivates me is that the cross is a public act with liberating consequences for the whole of humanity.

> The cross is the decisive victory of God's way in the world, and the resurrection is the empowering victory—the first sign of this new era.

We are called to carry the message of the cross with us in the world every day, as we, in Christ and by the power of the Spirit, reflect this new way of living in all its attractive freedom. And we have been shown what this new life of freedom can mean. It means love, forgiveness, service, and sacrifice—living for others rather than power-grabbing, self-actualization, and the cult of the self.

The Mark of Christ Crucified

The apostle Paul said he bore on his body the marks of Jesus (Gal. 6:17). This is a vivid image for us today given the explosive growth in tattoos worldwide. What used to be a discreet butterfly has become a bold and visible series of letters, images, and designs. Many celebrities have at least one tattoo, displayed for all to see, proclaiming or advocating some kind of message.

In much the same way, we carry the mark of Christ crucified with us wherever we go. We carry it unashamedly, not hidden or covered up. By the ways we engage with our colleagues, friends, families, and other people we meet, we reflect, as boldly as if it were physical, the image of Christ and the hallmarks of the new life initiated by the cross. A life of forgiveness, understanding, tolerance, and love, and, of course, a life that is utterly uncompromising in the face of evil.

This is the new kingdom that Jesus spoke of almost as a mantra in every encounter he had. As an integral part of our daily prayer routine, we pray for his kingdom, however strange, to come on earth.

I felt the power and the potential of this new kingdom most acutely in the great financial crisis when it seemed as if uncontrollable forces were at work in the world. Of course, the issues of the banking crisis were complex and difficult, but through it all I knew that it did not have to be that way. We could point to a better way of governing our finances. In my role as Gresham Professor of Commerce in the city of London, I was pleased to devote a series of lectures to reconnecting the financial world with its ethical foundations. I believe that the power of the cross enables Christians in every

> **The power of the cross enables Christians in every sphere of life to demonstrate that the world can be different from the prevailing narrative and indeed that it *is* different as a result of Christ's death.**

sphere of life to demonstrate that the world can be different from the prevailing narrative and indeed that it *is* different as a result of Christ's death.

Similarly, a few years ago, when the Occupy movement camped outside of St. Paul's Cathedral in a demonstration against the failures of capitalism, there was fear that violence would break out on the steps. The cathedral was closed as a precautionary measure. But the church stepped in to show there was another way.

I led a team on behalf of the bishop of London, aiming to mediate between those in the tents and the executives in the city to promote a dialogue that might ease the tension. London Connection, which I was honored to chair, grew out of that event. Its aim was to connect ethics and finance and to take on board the legitimate concerns of those demonstrating. For me, this is what the cross is about. It is not merely a place of forgiveness but a source of power for renewal and reconciliation. The cross, for all its barbaric inhumanity, liberates humanity to act as free agents in a hostile world. It has a resonance of genuine humanness that has not diminished through the ages, and it reminds us who and how we are called to be.

The Core Story of Humanity

We are not to reflect the cross in a self-satisfied or self-interested way but instead by demonstrating this new era of humanity, in which a passion for justice, executed through sacrificial service, has been enabled and made possible at every level and in every area of our society. The cross is the core story of humanity, and it is the special calling of Christians to make this core story real in our everyday lives.

Of course, there are times when this all seems like distant, empty, theoretical nonsense, when life's challenges are hard to understand, and when God seems to be a long way away. This is as true for you as it is for me. But I often come back to that day in my university room when I accepted Jesus into my life. I return to the moment when I realized that Jesus had died for me and that, because of this I would never again need to doubt that the gates of hell, powerful as they may be, would prevail against his love and grace in my life. Such freedom. Such extraordinary

> The cross is the core story of humanity, and it is the special calling of Christians to make this core story real in our everyday lives.

love. And such a powerful sense of calling to extend the knowledge of his love and grace, in whatever ways I would be able, to those I would encounter in the years ahead.

The story of Jesus' crucifixion at Calvary subverts the stories that have dominated the narrative of secular history and flies in the face of contemporary sensibilities. Stories of human strength, self-mastery, self-autonomy, self-realization, and human perfectibility are the order of the day.

We've adopted the idolatry entrusted in the "modernist trinity": First, the confident individual who says, "I am the master of my own making" and "I am the captain of my soul and will steer it as I will." Human beings have become kings and queens in their own self-constructed kingdoms, and we have exported this ethos to the rest of the world in the name of unrestrained capitalism and consumerism—and in our unlimited faith in education, science, and technology, trusting these to solve all our problems and bring about a universal peace.

Second, we have developed a tone of certainty about the world, as if our knowing is in some way objective and infallible. We have shut the door on God, and, in turn, tried to make ourselves God. The central claim of the recent book *Homo Deus*, by bestselling author Yuval Noah Harari, is that, in essence, human beings are the new gods. Through the data revolution, we have become the central controllers of life and the future shape of the world. We have an unparalleled ability to control the world around us, which is turning us into something new altogether: human gods. We no longer have a basis for constructing morality and the ethics of right and wrong, and instead we make pragmatic decisions based on human design and ingenuity. But these no longer hang on any absolutes.

The story of the cross subverts such "progress," which is shown to be irrelevant against the backdrop of our own stories. Our culture's currency is independence, and we are offered infinite possibilities to help us form our infinitely malleable identities, crowning our self-constructed images as the solution to all life's dilemmas and dysfunctions, and then changing it at will.

Like a screensaver on our computers, our postmodern selves are constantly changing into new configurations. For some, identity is formed through sexual promiscuity or experimenting with new religions or occult techniques. For others, it is shaped by climbing up the proverbial ladder in their careers. And, to be clear, there is nothing wrong with this per se, except when selfish ambition is the only motivator. Whichever method we use, and we may try all of them at some point, the culture's view holds that the secret of the universe is within us, that we have a spark of the divine deep down inside, and the aim is to be true to that spark and follow that star wherever it leads.

Third, and perhaps above all, we have a new mythology of cultural progress and relational intelligence. Cyberspace and virtual reality have afforded us the means to constantly self-create and to seek recognition for this auto-created self by joining virtual communities. Even on the Internet, no less in our physical neighborhoods, we move toward others who are just like us. But in virtual communities—where there is no need for the give-and-take of real relationships—our identity is connected to how many followers we have, rather than to the messy business of real relationships of mutual help, service, and kindness. And, of course, our onus is to be the one who others follow.

We have replaced authentic community with online popularity. Preferring Facebook to face-to-face contact, "instamacy" over intimacy, we are drawn to technologies that provide the illusion of companionship without the demands of relationship.

The negative consequences of all this are quite clear: As we zoom out of these social constructs, it is not surprising that the symbol of the cross is met with such disdain and resistance. The person of Jesus—his life and his death—challenges the power of self-actualization and self-reliance and flies in the face of human independence. All these things—things that center wholly on the self—are absent at the cross of Christ where the self is laid down for the sake of others. By the tests of self-actualization, of self-reliance, of independence, he lost the battle.

One of the principal effects of the cross was to break the power of idolatry. Idol worship was replaced on the cross by the freedom to live in the light of a new relationship with the true God. Idols—the veneration of self is perhaps the most powerful idol in our world today—destroy our true humanity. The cross restores the fullness of life by breaking the compulsive demands of the dominant idols

---

in our world. The cross tells us that these are not the things in which our identity is held together, but rather that in Christ "all things hold together" (Col. 1:17).

From the moment I first heard Tim Hughes's recent song "The Cross Stands," I was struck by the great truth it was celebrating. It is an uplifting song of great celebration. I often repeat the refrain, particularly in times of confusion or when, at work, it seems as if people are determined to tear each other apart in argument and confrontation. In these times it is great to remember the towering visibility of the cross and its broad and deep reach into every corner of life, however fraught or fractious.

> Idol worship was replaced on the cross by the freedom to live in the light of a new relationship with the true God.

The workplace can be one of the hardest and darkest places on earth. I always try to remember that even though work might be dead in its apparent futility, the cross reaches to that extreme place of despair, disappointment, and darkness. And this is true also for the despair wrought by destructive relationships, experiences of profound injustice and rejection, or ongoing illness and bereavement.

Kings tend to reign through victory, yet this King appeared to have lost as he breathed his last on the cross to the jeers of the gathered crowd. But the man they thought was a loser turned out to be the Victor: the Savior, the Liberator of humanity, among whom he lived and whose agonies and joys he shared and whose future he now shapes. What then is this victory that turns a loser into a king?

The victory is the fact that the cross is the end of history. It marks the end of humanity's need to search for God. That defining quest, ongoing for millennia, has ended. The cross is the climax of God reaching out for mankind. It is the definitive point of history. And it marks a break in time. First, God's actions were seen in the world through a defined group of people—Israel—in a specific place called Palestine, through intermediaries, priests, and scholars. Then, the angle of the lens broadened, becoming wider and wider, as it opened to "the priesthood of all believers" and the invitation to a restored relationship with God was offered to all humankind.

As history ends, the new creation, or the new world, is inaugurated through the cross. When we think of the cross, we may be meditating on the death of Christ, but his life, death, and resurrection are an inseparable unity. He died. It seemed like the end. The victor appeared to be death. But he was victorious, and he defeated the powers of darkness by bringing new life to all creation.

It has been the claim of Christ and of Christians throughout the ages that Christ died for us, standing in our place at the moment of God's judgment. Jesus took our place and with it our death and our sins, and we took his place, gaining his acceptance and his righteousness in the eyes of God. We do not have an accuser but an advocate, one who took our punishment and paid the ultimate price with his own blood. And, in so doing, Christ inaugurated a new community of freed people.

> **We do not have an accuser but an advocate, one who took our punishment and paid the ultimate price with his own blood.**

Jesus pleads our case on the basis that he paid the price.

The Ultimate Victory

Jesus' death was not a defeat but the ultimate victory—a victory over all the powers of darkness, over all the determinist forces of sex, power, and self-fulfillment that claim to govern our lives. "And having disarmed the powers and authorities, he made a public spectacle of them, triumphing over them by the cross" (Col. 2:15). The victory over these destructive powers, which was won on the cross, was sealed in the resurrection. He rose again to underline that he had conquered the human delusion that death is the end.

Is it surprising that from Jesus' greatest act of love would flow his greatest power? The life of the Christian is not the imitation of a dead hero who lost. Rather, the Christian lives in Jesus, and Jesus lives in the Christian through the power of the Holy Spirit in the new world order he established through his death. To me that isn't the mark of a "loser" but of a Savior who lives in the power of his Spirit, and who enables us to live each day enjoying the freedom of life, without the fear of death, and with the hope of resurrection life. We may anxiously count our online followers, and we may search around for new, inspiring people to follow on our Twitter accounts, but here surely is the One worth following above all others.

Jesus rose again to underline that he had conquered the human delusion that death is the end.

All that was written in the Law of Moses, the Prophets, and the Psalms has been fulfilled, and the strangest and most radical of kings, the King of kings, has set us free to lead lives of fulfillment and purpose as we set about building his strange kingdom here on earth.

A Time to Meditate

Music

- "The Cross Stands," Tim Hughes
- "Ubi Caritas," Ola Gjeilo

Reflect

- Jesus died for us in one mighty and definitive reorientation. He put us first and himself last. We can choose to feed the hungry demands of the self and we will never be satisfied. Or we can feed the hunger—literal, spiritual, psychological, and emotional—all around us. Now is as good a time as any to decide which it will be. Will you be reoriented by his love to live for love?

- The threefold *cross*, *resurrection*, and *giving of the Spirit* is the engine we need to be released into fulfilled lives of sacrifice, service, love, and purpose—to be agents of change in the world. But first, perhaps this is the moment to ask God to come and bring about the change in you that will enable you to be the change you pray for.

- The cross is supremely about life—the new life we can enjoy *together* in Jesus Christ. He died for you, yes, but, most of all, he died *for us*. The culture is all about me, but the Christian journey is both personal and communal. What is God calling you to do, individually and with your community of fellow travelers?

Prayer

The cross stands above it all. Lord, today, I want to be reoriented. I stand, with all who follow you, at the foot of the towering cross, and I allow its power to reach wide and deep into every corner of my life that I might be oriented away from the self and reach out with power, purpose, love, and grace wherever you may call me, amen.

NINE

FLOURISHING

"The thief comes only to steal and kill and destroy; I have come that they may have life, and have it to the full."

—John 10:10

THE CROSS STARTED THE REGIME CHANGE AND THE
resurrection underwrote it, indicating that something new had
been birthed. It doesn't make sense to capture the cross as just one
milestone event, nor to try to understand it as a separate stand-
alone scene unrelated to the life of Jesus—and consequently our
own. We cannot wrench his death out of the context of his life and
resurrection, nor our own.

It must have been just another work-
day for the Roman soldiers on that Friday
that we now call "good." They obeyed
instructions from Pilate to make sure that
Jesus was in fact dead, that there could
be no doubt in anybody's mind that Jesus
had breathed his last. The soldiers assured
Pilate that he had. To the soldiers Jesus
was like any other criminal or insurrec-
tionist. As they thrust the spear into Jesus'
side, it removed all debate and doubt

> The cross started the regime change and the resurrection underwrote it, indicating that something new had been birthed.

of his death. After all, the Romans knew their job, and their job
was finished and well done. They handed over Jesus' body at the
request of Joseph of Arimathea and the religious leader Nicodemus
who was with him.

Joseph and Nicodemus were both men who held significant
positions of power and would have been wealthy. And I love the
fact that they were there, as ever business people are, to do the

practical necessities: the preparation and burial of Jesus' body. Not a core disciple was in sight! But these two men would have traded all they had for one breath from Jesus, one movement, any sign of life. He had answered their fervent prayers for the expected Messiah to come. And now they attended to him in death.

We know the soldiers and Pilate wanted him dead, and for his death to send a clear message from the Roman Empire to anyone who thought they might follow suit. But how much more did Joseph and Nicodemus want him alive? They must have yearned to turn back the clock to a week earlier, when Jesus would have been sitting and eating with them. As they wiped and cleaned the matted stains of blood from his beard, I imagine their sense of brokenness and despair. As they prepared him for burial, I picture them clinging to his claims of Messiahship as they searched for life. But to no avail. They lifted up his body, carefully balancing the weight, and carried it to be placed in Joseph's tomb.

When Joseph and Nicodemus left Jesus in the tomb, a process would begin in which a Roman seal was set on the rock at the entrance. In the first century, to protect a letter and to make sure the content of the correspondence was secure, the letter was sealed. It assured that it was secure and confirmed it would be received without being tampered with. It was the ancient-day equivalent of the modern-day business transactions that I so often find myself in. I have signed many contracts, my signature confirming my identity and the integrity of the transaction.

A similar sealing occurred at Jesus' tomb. Apparatus were applied to the entrance of the tomb and placed together with a substance similar to wax, which then had the Roman seal placed upon it. It was a serious reminder to everyone concerned that Rome had won! Jesus was not who he claimed to be. Case dismissed. The contents of this tomb belong to the Roman Empire. For three full days, the tomb was sealed, an impenetrable fortress, protected by Roman rule and the imperial regime.

But then, as the silence of Saturday passed, Sunday was here. Jesus' heart valves opened, and his chest expanded. His joints began to bend, his fingers to twitch. As the rest of the empire woke up on Sunday morning and turned their calendars to just another day, the dead body of Jesus inflated with breath and "just another day" became a pivot about which history would turn. Jesus, the man who had been locked up in death, burst to life, and a new, strange kingdom was born—a new order of grace in which those who were dead in sin could be raised to life in him. Christ had resurrected. The celebration could begin.

And no one articulates the celebration better than Paul: "Therefore, if anyone is in Christ, the new creation has come: The old has gone, the new is here!" (2 Cor. 5:17). Jesus' death on the cross not only signals but brings about the end of the world as we have known it, and the resurrection not only signals but brings about the beginning of the new world. This is the culmination of one period of history and the inauguration of a new age. But how do we today respond to this extraordinary ancient story?

> Jesus, the man who had been locked up in death, burst to life, and a new, strange kingdom was born—a new order of grace in which those who were dead in sin could be raised to life in him.

I wonder how we would have reacted had we been there. For Mary Magdalene, a celebration was the last thing on her mind as she walked toward the tomb on that Sunday morning. The Jewish leaders could celebrate with an air of relief that Jesus was out of the picture. The soldiers could celebrate that their work was done and that it truly was finished. Another day, another denarius. But Mary had nothing to celebrate. The last few days had brought her only excruciating pain. She had heard the leaders shout for Jesus' blood. She had been amid the chaos of the crowd as they shouted, "Crucify him! Crucify him!" (Luke 23:21). She had seen the whip rip the skin off his back with thirty-nine lashes. She had winced and looked on in horror as the thorns sliced his brow, and she had wept at the weight of the cross that Jesus had to carry and the significance of what that represented. Jesus was crucified, died, and was buried.

Then, "early on the first day of the week, while it was still dark, Mary Magdalene went to the tomb and saw that the stone had been removed from the entrance" (John 20:1). How would we have responded? Mary's response was to run to Peter and John and tell them someone had taken Jesus' body out of the tomb. They ran to the tomb and found it empty (vv. 2–10).

> Now Mary stood outside the tomb crying. As she wept, she bent over to look into the tomb and saw two angels in white, seated where Jesus' body had been, one at the head and the other at the foot.
>
> They asked her, "Woman, why are you crying?"
>
> "They have taken my Lord away," she said, "and I don't know where they have put him." At this, she turned around and saw Jesus standing there, but she did not realize that it was Jesus. (vv. 11–14)

What pathos there is in the words "my Lord"—her very own Lord, the man who did so much for her and whom she loved to follow. Jesus could have immediately let Mary know who he was, but instead he asked her, "Woman, why are you crying? Who is it you are looking for?" (v. 15).

> Thinking he was the gardener, she said, "Sir, if you have carried him away, tell me where you have put him, and I will get him."
> Jesus said to her, "Mary." (vv. 15–16)

The familiar tone gripped her heart, and then she recognized him. "She turned toward him and cried out in Aramaic, 'Rabboni!' (which means 'Teacher')" (v. 16).

We are told that when the women met the resurrected Jesus, they "came to him, clasped his feet and worshiped him" (Matt. 28:9). But what about the response of his other disciples? What about Peter, who had once walked fearlessly on the water toward Jesus, but who also had hurried away from him into hiding after denying he even knew Jesus? To deny him once would have been pitiful, but to deny him three times was surely shameful. When questioned further and fearful for his own safety, Peter had called down curses on himself, swearing, "I don't know the man!" (Matt. 26:74).

And so, as Jesus rose from the dead, Peter was left with his guilt and his sorrow, perhaps wondering whether Jesus would return for someone like him, someone who had messed up by choice—and not just once. I am sure I am not alone in wondering the same. Don't we wonder sometimes whether we deserve to be disqualified from his love?

Perhaps we can relate to the volume of his boasting. Perhaps, now, with Peter, we can feel the remorse and regret of our shame. It was when the rooster crowed that Peter was pierced by his shame as his shortcomings were highlighted and exposed. And there are times when we, too, weep as Peter wept. And perhaps some of us need to hear the rooster crow to reposition us, as Peter would be gloriously renewed, released, and regifted by God.

Perhaps some of us need to hear the rooster crow to reposition us, as Peter would be gloriously renewed, released, and regifted by God.

But for now, Peter went back to his boat and back to fishing. We know why he went to Galilee: he'd been told that Jesus would meet the disciples there. But the arranged meeting place was a mountain, not a lake. We haven't seen Peter fish since he left his nets to follow Jesus. So why did he go fishing? Maybe the disciples were just hungry. But I think it was more than that.

When we have gone wrong, it is easy to be tempted to return to our former mind-sets. It is easy to forget that God loves and accepts us not because we are perfect but because of Jesus' perfect sacrifice, because of grace.

Jesus answered the question of whether Peter was still worthy of his love—and he answered it powerfully by the Sea of Tiberias. He answered it for Peter, in the middle of the lake basin, and he does so for you and me. Jesus didn't perform a miracle and part the waters or turn the boat to gold. Jesus acted in a much more significant manner and in a way that would leave a mark on Peter's life and remain etched in his memory forever. He invited Peter to join him on the shore for breakfast. No doubt there would be many more powerful moments with Jesus from then on, but the Bible records how there was a large catch of fish, followed by Peter's revelation that it was Jesus his friend and the Messiah that caused him to plunge into waters of the lake. Jesus was waiting for Peter and the other disciples there, and the man who three days earlier had been through the fire of suffering, prepared a fire where he was boiling fish and making lunch for his friends. How human, how normal, yet the whole scene awakens a picture of divinity and victory.

Here was Jesus, flesh-and-blood Jesus, who had said, "Look at my hands and my feet. It is I myself! Touch me and see; a ghost does not have flesh and bones, as you see I have" (Luke 24:39). This was a body real enough to have walked from Jerusalem, to have set up the fire, and—according to the Gospel of Luke—to eat a piece of broiled fish in the disciples' presence. This was a real body. But Jesus' body was different, so substantial that walls couldn't stop him. His body was real but also glorified. It was a heavenly body and, as Mark said, Jesus "appeared in another form" (16:12 ESV).

Here was the resurrected Jesus, by the side of the lake; here was the defeater of death and the grave, the ruler of the heavens. And what did he do? He invited his friends to sit down and share a meal with him. Jesus is who he claimed to be—the man who had the courage to sacrifice his life for the forgiveness of sins—and he has the power he claimed to have. And he invites us, as he invited Peter, to sit with him. We are all welcome, even if, like Peter, we feel we've totally messed up beyond redemption. The undeserving sit alongside the deserving at Jesus' table. He met them not in a

> He met them not in a temple or a synagogue, but in their place of work, in their everyday routine, and there he sanctified their daily lives—and ours with theirs.

temple or a synagogue, but in their place of work, in their everyday routine, and there he sanctified their daily lives—and ours with theirs—by drawing them into a meal together and using some of the fruit of their labor, the fish they had caught, to feed them.

What will it be for us as we are invited to that same meal: yes or no? Brennan Manning wrote:

> My YES to the fullness of divinity embodied in the present risenness of Jesus is scary because it is so personal. In desolation and abandonment . . . in loneliness and fear, in the awareness of the resident pharisee, and in the antics of the imposter, YES is a bold word not to be taken lightly or spoken frivolously.
>
> This YES is an act of faith, a decisive, wholehearted response of my whole being to the risen Jesus present beside me, before me, around me, and within me; a cry of confidence that my faith in Jesus provides security not only in the face of death but in the face of a worse threat posed by my own malice; a word that must be said not just once but repeated over and over again in the ever-changing landscape of life.[1]

Our yes is the start to a new life of flourishing in Christ.

In the twenty-first-century maelstrom of competing demands and whirlwind pressures, we so desperately need the anchor of the risen Lord, a stillness at the center, where we can acknowledge that in Christ "all things hold together" (Col. 1:17). As I write this book, I feel an urgency about asking you, perhaps for the first time, or perhaps in a new way, how you are going to respond to the empty tomb. How will you, on behalf of yourself and indeed on behalf of your community—your church, your city—respond to this strange kingdom where even death is defeated in the most glorious way?

Facebook or Faithbook?

The founder and pioneer of the social network platform Facebook, Mark Zuckerberg, recently published his manifesto for building a new global Facebook community to mark the milestone of Facebook reaching two billion active users worldwide. Founders of global movements often want to create an ethos for their followers that gives them a greater purpose and fulfilment beyond mere functionality. Zuckerberg's ambitious and ardent manifesto aims to draw his two billion Facebook users into building a more intentional global community.[2]

With that foundation, the post proceeds to focus on how Facebook endeavors to engage in developing the social infrastructure for such a community, explaining how it will support us, keep us safe, inform us, keep us engaged, and bring about inclusion for all. This manifesto was triggered by statistics showing that a large percentage of our population lacks a sense of hope for the future. There seems to be a lack of community and connection to something greater than ourselves. Mark Zuckerberg has seized this opportunity to challenge two billion Facebook users to become, in addition to being users, active Facebook participants in a shared global vision for the improvement of humanity. It's a great vision. A similar number of people across the world profess to hold faith in Jesus Christ and the book that contains his manifesto.

Two founders with their manifestos. Both have at their core the desire to see a community formed and working together. Facebook wants to give people the power to build a global community. And it is a formidable tool for good. But where does this power come from? What is its source? If it is just internally generated, it cannot be sustained and cannot have the strength to fulfill our deepest longings for community.

In light of what Zuckerberg has encouraged, do we as Christians therefore face a choice? Is it Facebook or Faithbook? Is it one or the other? Do we have to separate ourselves from the world and this community, in case it dilutes what we hold to be dear and true? The answer is no. It's both. We are called to live as a radical community, agents for change in both worlds. But with one enormous difference: the power to bring about the changes we long for.

We are empowered to influence and change things, taking and reshaping, reinterpreting, refashioning, and remodeling a half-painted picture as Zuckerberg has done. We get to be a community that can fill in the colors. Zuckerberg's manifesto for building a new community, as noble and as positive as it is, can only create a digital world. But the church is a real community of human beings: a physical presence on the ground, digitally but above all humanly empowered, to extend the kingdom of God as we flourish in him.

This new community is "a community of friends," formed from Jesus' great love, which led him to lay down his life for his friends (John 15:13). This community of which we are a part is the fulfillment of the plan of salvation. What the cross secured, the resurrection cemented and the Spirit delivered: the power to bring about actual change to the real lives of all people and to realign the ways of the world with God's purpose for the world.

Resurrection is thus God's power at work. The threat of daily external decay and death is met by daily inner renewal through the Spirit. Herein lies the power of the resurrection in establishing and invigorating this new community of faith. Here is the sustaining power to equip us to flourish amid turmoil in the world and in our daily lives. Paul wrote that the same power that raised Christ from the dead is given to us.

The resurrection underwrites this radical newness we now have. We are to live "for him who died [for us] and was raised again." The cross and the resurrection always go together. Such a way of living is possible because for everyone who is "in Christ, the new creation has come" (2 Cor. 5:15, 17). That is, those who are in Christ find themselves drawn into a new order energized by the power of the new era as Christ makes all things new through the resurrection. The resurrection models a new way of doing life, a way in which hope is restored, people are renewed, and the community of faith is recreated.

A Spirit-Filled Community

God's new age has broken into the old one, and heaven and earth have collided together in a fresh way, creating a world full of possibilities and a new power that leaves the old power lying helpless on the ground. It is as if the clocks have gone forward without warning, and the morning has come before we're ready for it. The alarm has gone off and God's new world—the world of the tripartite cross-resurrection-Holy Spirit—has begun and we're invited to get up and be a part of it. This is a new kind of life, a resurrection life that is unexpected and ongoing, formed within a new community. Jesus' death

> The resurrection underwrites this radical newness we now have. We are to live "for him who died [for us] and was raised again."

transforms our world by reuniting the children of God in a global community where no boundary between them can be a barrier.

Paul wrote that "the righteousness of God through faith in Jesus Christ [is] for all who believe" (Rom. 3:22 ESV). A panoramic view from creation to where we are now occupied Paul's thoughts in Romans 3:25–30, which speaks of the same theme: God will be faithful to his people, God will always bring to pass what he has promised, and God will bring together all people through the death and resurrection of Jesus. Paul made it clear in his writings that he had a picture of inclusivity for all people when this resurrection event happened. He wrote: "For there is no difference between Jew and Gentile—the same Lord is Lord of all and richly blesses all who call on him" (Rom. 10:12).

Without the resurrection, the hostile boundary lines between all people groups still remains; with the resurrection, a new community is formed centered around Jesus. When Jesus and his resurrection power is integrated into how we see and understand his death, we find ourselves compelled to explore this diverse, redeemed community of people, living out a life of faith in obedience to the service of Jesus.

Paul made an additional bold claim as he told the church in Corinth that because of the resurrection "your labor in the Lord is not in vain" (1 Cor. 15:58). The resurrection is the foretaste of the fulfillment of the new kingdom, and we can bring its power into our workplaces, homes, schools, and universities—wherever we meet people. But the resurrection is incomplete without the continuing presence of the Spirit of God equipping, releasing, and calling us into this new relationship of love in action in the world around us—without regard to race or creed or gender, or anything else that might divide person from person.

Pentecost comes not simply to regenerate individuals but to recreate a community of faith in which the will of God manifests itself in worship and fellowship and in intentional actions in the world. The Spirit is not given to make us more spiritual but to make us fully human. Irenaeus, the great second-century theologian, said that the "glory of God is a living man."[3] We find at Pentecost the divine intention of God's work on the cross: the creation of a community of faith in which and through which humans will be restored to union with God and communion with others for the good of the world.

As Zuckerberg's manifesto aims to achieve social inclusivity by digital means, a significant feature of the Pentecostal Spirit is the power to transcend, to break down boundaries, and to expand the people of God. The first part of the book of Acts records the history of the first Jewish-Christian community breaking down boundaries to expand into a more inclusive community of faith. We see the members of this faith community working out the practice of the gospel in a way that might include more and more people. We watch them learning how the faithfulness of God might extend first to the Samaritans, then to the Ethiopian eunuch, and then, through Peter, into the Gentile world, and finally, through Paul, into a full-scale missional focus on Gentiles, so that all people might be part of the universal redemptive designs of God.

If anything is certain, it is that the earliest Jewish-Christian community did not know what to make of the expansiveness of this community of faith, but they knew that the Spirit was giving its members the power to overcome their own hesitations. God doesn't give us the Holy Spirit to let us put our feet up and wait for heaven. No, the point of the Spirit is to enable those who follow Jesus to take the news that he is Lord into all the world: to proclaim that he has won the victory over the forces of evil; that a new world has opened up; and that we are to help bring this new world about. He enables us to understand the world we work in and to help redirect it to its true roots, as created by God.

God doesn't give us the Holy Spirit to let us put our feet up and wait for heaven.

Pentecost empowers us to be restored in all four directions: with God, with self, with others, and with the world. Pentecost crystallizes God's intent at the cross: to create a community of faith wherein the will of God is actualized in our day-to-day lives, a community whose common goal is to bring about justice and to fight against evil. And the gates to this new community are wide open to all. This community isn't limited to the noble cause of digital engagement and connectivity; rather it is a redemptive group of people who seek nothing less than the restoration of all things.

God's promise is that "you will receive power when the Holy Spirit comes on you; and you will be my witnesses in Jerusalem, and in all Judea and Samaria, and to the ends of the earth" (Acts 1:8). The power we receive from God will enable the members of this new community to change not only individual lives but also society. This manifesto compels us to love the world, fractured as it is, and to commit ourselves to the task of fighting injustice— whether campaigning against modern-day slavery, or for the rights of the poor and marginalized, or for the well-being of the planet.

Resurrection Hope

There have been many symbols over the years that have sought to capture the essence and nature of the resurrection hope we have.

Resurrection was often symbolized by a butterfly, as it emerged from the chrysalis-tomb. Another ancient symbol is the scarab beetle, which appeared to emerge from the dust out of nothing. In fact, one of the ancient patristic scholars talked about Jesus the scarab, who comes out of the dust—out of nothing—in a kind of spontaneous creation.[4] And the phoenix rising to life from the fire was also used to symbolize Jesus' resurrection. But my favorite is the peacock, the most beautiful image of early Christianity, found engraved in the catacombs. The peacock sheds its feathers, but each year the feathers return brighter, more beautiful, and more glorious than the year before. More than any symbol, however, it is every act of love, every act of kindness, every encouragement one to another, every act of care and nurture that will best show others the resurrection power of God breaking into the new creation.

I remember that soon after I came to faith, someone told me that one of the atheist philosophers of the time, Marghanita Laski, had described Jesus as the freest man who had ever lived. And this had a profound effect on my life as I determined to explore more deeply and experience more personally his transformational power. Jesus, who washed the feet of others and allowed others to wash his feet. Jesus, who changed what was ugly into what was beautiful. Jesus, who was passionate about his cause. Jesus, who was willing to shed his own blood but never willing to shed the blood of others. Jesus, who lived in peace with God, and who would enable all of us to "have peace with God through our Lord Jesus Christ, through whom we have gained access by faith into this grace in which we now stand" (Rom. 5:1–2).

Surely all of us are inspired by the thought of having peace with God. This book follows on from *Know Your Why*, a book I wrote to try and help Christians find and fulfill their calling. I believe that this is the greatest pastoral need of our age. A generation is growing up stressed out and burned out, facing a pervasive identity crisis as they seek to find purpose in their lives within a rapidly changing digital world. It is a time of both intense demand and unimaginable opportunity, as the tech revolution changes almost every aspect of our daily lives. It is into this world that the cross of Jesus speaks most powerfully.

Jesus knew his why. He knew where he came from and where he was going (John 8:14). And where he was going was to Jerusalem to a particular place for a particular purpose: to die for us. The purpose of his death was, yes, to restore our relationship with God by dealing with our sins, but also—and this is vitally important for our lives today—his death was a unique calling to bring about a new way of living for all humankind. And not only for Christians. He overcame the usurped rule of the idolatrous power structures of evil to enable a new world order to take root. A new world order in which the whole of humanity has the opportunity to be restored to its rightful relationship with its Creator, rather than being slaves to a superpower of evil.

I often ask people, "What is your core story?" The core story of your life is whatever your passion is, and it is like an acorn within you. I believe there is within every Christian a God-implanted core story. An idea ready to germinate, a hope about to flourish, a song ready to be sung, an aspiration about to be fulfilled. It could flourish and become a great oak, powerful enough to resist the storms of life. Or it could remain a sapling, never maturing, but bending and swaying in the wind.

What wakes me up in the morning is the

Jesus knew his why. He knew where he came from and where he was going.

idea that in some small way I can help equip and release the next generation to write strong and powerful narratives in their lives, which will help change the world. The verse that sums up my core story says that "even when I'm old and gray [and I think I am at least gray!], do not forsake me, my God, till I declare your power to the next generation, your mighty acts to all who are to come" (Ps. 71:18).

What is your core story?

For us to live a fulfilled life and to flourish within the full meaning of the resurrection, we need to ask the Holy Spirit to awaken us to our core stories and to charge them with his power. We will remain saplings if we try to act on our willpower alone, but an encounter with the resurrected power of Jesus will enable our core stories to mature into strong oaks, strengthening with the years and growing new branches in new seasons.

A few months ago, I had the great privilege of being part of a group who spent two hours with Pope Francis. In the meeting, someone asked the Pope why he wasn't living in the papal apartments. The grand and secluded papal apartments have been home to Popes since the seventh century. The Pope replied: "I can't live without people. It's a personal thing—my mother made me that way." I found this fascinating. The Pope, one of the most influential people on the planet, has a core story: *people*.

> We need to ask the Holy Spirit to awaken us to our core stories and to charge them with his power.

In the current chapter of the story, he is Pope. But many other chapters came first, and there were no doubt twists and turns, complex plots perhaps, crossroads, tangents even. We may not all be Pope, but we are each called to live out our core story in the light of the resurrection story, through the power of the Holy

Spirit. And we do so knowing that we are those who "have gained access by faith into this grace in which we now stand" (Rom. 5:2).

As we allow the grace of God to flow through the pages of our core stories, written in us by God, then the frustration, anxiety, disappointments, and failures of our lives become bearable, and we begin to flourish as human beings. We flourish because we know that the same power that saw Christ raised from the dead is working in us to write something of worth in our lives, even in times of distress.

We need to get real. The world has persuaded us of a narrative in which the plot turns around striving, success, goals, achievement, and performance. But we must live a different cross-shaped narrative. In many ways the cross is a glorious defeat, a glorious injustice, a glorious failure. And unlike most stories, this one, energized by the resurrection power of Christ, will have no ending. If you are reading this and thinking that your core story has hit a dead end, it hasn't. We each can take our core story and plant it into Jesus' core story, the greatest one ever told—a narrative of love for us, our society, and the world.

We should think of the Beatitudes not primarily as offering a blessing *to* those who are described but *through* them to the world.

We each can take our core story and plant it into Jesus' core story, the greatest one ever told—a narrative of love for us, our society, and the world.

Those who intercede for the world's needs and groan for its wrongs are those who fight "the good fight of the faith" (1 Tim. 6:12). We fight this fight and defeat the powers of death not with more evil or more deaths, but with the power of love, and we do so until the second coming of the King and the consummation of the kingdom.

We must be encouraged that many blessings of this strange kingdom are available now. The decisive battle against sin and death has been fought and Christ is victorious in and through his death, burial, and resurrection but the war wages on, and the battle is not over. Sin must be resisted and we must use the weapons available to us, to equip us to stand until that day when Jesus returns to bring with him the truly new heaven and earth, and where there will be no place for the alien forces of evil as Jesus waits for his enemies to be made his footstool (Heb. 10:13).

This strange kingdom has been inaugurated, and it has arrived. We may only have signposts pointing to it rather than a full panoramic photograph of how it might look, but the King has come. He has sacrificed himself for our sin and is sitting at the Father's right hand. His righteousness is available to us by faith. We have the power to partner with God to bring in his kingdom on a day-to-day basis and to live our lives from a place of acceptance and assurance that we will find our ultimate fulfillment in him.

Our work in this life is practice for our work in the coming life. In one sense, what we do now matters, all by itself. But, in another sense, it's practice. The philosopher Dallas Willard said this life is "training for reigning." As cheesy as it sounds, Willard was spot on. Right now, we are learning the skills we'll need forever in God's new world. In fact, the Bible substantiates such claims, as it talks about God giving citizens of this strange kingdom a calling to rule, to look after his creation and make it flourish, and—after a long, drawn-out detour through the generations of human history—the Bible ends with such a vision:

"[He] has made us to be a kingdom of priests" (Rev. 1:6 PAR).
"I will give the right to sit with me on my throne" (Rev. 3:21).

"They shall reign on the earth" (Rev. 5:10 ESV).
"They will reign for ever and ever" (Rev. 22:5).

And so our future hope isn't only that Jesus will rule the world; it is also that we will rule right at his side in this strange kingdom. As Paul put it, "If we endure, we will also reign with him" (2 Tim. 2:12). God is looking for people he can rule his world with, and right now, every single day, wherever we are, we are becoming those kinds of people. And so, as each one of us takes up our cross daily to follow him (Luke 9:23), there will come a time when this strange kingdom will not be strange at all. It will be the sublime kingdom of our Lord and King.

We get a picture of this in the final book of the Bible, the Revelation of John:

Then I looked and heard the voice of many angels, numbering thousands upon thousands, and ten thousand times ten thousand. They encircled the throne and the living creatures and the elders. In a loud voice they were saying:

"Worthy is the Lamb, who was slain,
to receive power and wealth and wisdom and strength
and honor and glory and praise!"

Then I heard every creature in heaven and on earth and under the earth and on the sea, and all that is in them, saying:

"To him who sits on the throne and to the Lamb
be praise and honor and glory and power,
for ever and ever!"

(Rev. 5:11–13)

One of my favorite stories is about the French composer, Olivier Messiaen, and his famous piece "Quartet for the End of Time," which was written in the winter of 1941. Messiaen had been captured by the Nazi regime and put in Stalag 8-A, a prisoner-of-war camp in Gorlitz, Germany. While in prison, facing a brutally cruel lifestyle, he spent time reading the four Gospels and the book of Revelation. As a follower of Jesus, he was filled with hope for the world, right in the middle of the hell and terror of his circumstances.

When Messiaen realized there were three other famous musicians in the camp, he found four instruments: a cello with a missing string, a beaten-up old violin, a well-worn clarinet, and a piano with keys missing or stuck together, and he composed a piece of chamber music. Someone later called it "the most ethereally beautiful music of the twentieth century." The musicians first played it in January, right in the middle of the camp, to hundreds of prisoners and guards, in the freezing cold air. Messiaen later said, "The cold was excruciating, the Stalag buried under snow, the four performers played on broken down instruments but never have I had an audience who listened with such rapt attention."[5]

As I reflect upon that story I can't think of a more dramatic or fitting picture of the nature of the strange kingdom, whose music cannot be contained but breaks out amid the pain of this world. We are all less-than-perfect instruments. But God makes the best of our brokenness and creates in the resurrection the most sublime triumph of wholeness over brokenness. The broken body of Christ on Good Friday becomes the restored body on Easter Sunday. We are the people of the future who bring hope to the present.

And the hope is that, as we do whatever it is we do, in whatever environment we are called to, people will see our lives and shivering in the cold they will come a little closer, listen to the music we play, and start to see that here within the chaos and confusion of life on earth something new has been birthed. And, as they gather in, perhaps they will sense that a strange kingdom is seeping up through the ground, present yet future, flourishing but not consummated, breaking into people's lives and revealing the King of this strange kingdom: Jesus Christ.

A Time to Meditate

Music

- "Resurrecting," Elevation Worship
- "Praise to the Eternity of Jesus," *Quartet for the End of Time*, Olivier Messiaen

Reflect

- As the book ends, this is a good moment to stand with Peter and bring to God anything you've said or done or thought that is still eating away at you. If we find ourselves weeping with Peter, so will we find ourselves renewed, released, and regifted by God, as Peter was. I wonder what will come next for you. Be full of anticipation.
- The glory of God is a human being fully alive, as Peter was when he stood restored and redeemed to preach at Pentecost. The power he received is the power you

will receive so that you might flourish to the full. If you haven't already, ask God to confirm your core story. Are you ready to plant it into Jesus' core story?

- I wonder which symbol you relate to—butterfly, scarab, or phoenix. But by his Spirit all of us can become like the peacock, whose feathers grow brighter and more beautiful each year. This is the journey we are on, and it will take us from here into eternity. Are you ready for the ride?

Prayer

Lord, the tomb was empty because you'd risen from the dead. I choose to die with you and to be raised to new life with you. Thank you that, whether we deserve it or not, we are invited to sit at your table, restored to union with you and communion with those around us for the good of the world in which we live and for your glory, amen.

ACKNOWLEDGMENTS

I AM VERY GRATEFUL TO NICKY GUMBEL, VICAR OF Holy Trinity Brompton, for inviting me to speak at the Good Friday services at HTB. The meditations from these services form the basis of this book.

I would like to thank the various people who have been instrumental in the writing and completion of this book.

Rob Wall has worked tirelessly on research; he has been a great encourager. Jo Glen and Alice Goodwin-Hudson have edited the book meticulously and graciously. They have had to accommodate the eccentric working hours and travel schedule of my day job. Brad Lomenick, Tom Andrew, and Claire Elwin have worked with me to refine the presentation of the material and Rob McDonald has checked for heresies.

The team at Emanate Books, Joel Kneedler, Janene MacIvor, Joey Paul, Cody Van Ryn, Kristen Andrews, and Mallory Collins have been enthusiastic and encouraging from the start. They have worked round the clock to get the manuscript delivered in time. I am so grateful for your support, and for believing in the book.

ACKNOWLEDGMENTS

I am particularly grateful to my wife, Fi, and my four children, who have been endlessly patient with me, and have regularly challenged my deliberations and reflections.

I want to thank Nicky Gumbel and Nicky Lee for their friendship. Our lives were transformed at university more than forty years ago when we discovered the liberating message of the cross. We have journeyed together ever since then. Their support and encouragement has been unquantifiable.

QUOTES TO PONDER

Introduction

- To claim that Jesus' death and apparent defeat could be disguised as the ultimate victory would be very strange thinking indeed.
- What does the cross mean for ordinary Christians, for you and for me, in our everyday lives—at work, at home, in our communities?
- Even the darkness of depression that hits so many of us does not reach the depth of [Jesus'] suffering.
- [The cross] is the outward visual [or visible] sign of the Christian faith, a sign of hope for every human being. Even the critics can't ignore it.
- Jesus faced his death squarely in the eye, and this gives me courage to face the most hostile situations.
- My prayer is that the puzzle of the power of the cross will draw you into a closer encounter with the risen Jesus Christ.

Chapter One: Foolishness

- Jesus' definition of power, in the strange kingdom he inaugurates on earth, is something new and perhaps shocking—a genuine alternative to the political power constructs of this world.
- The symbol of the cross hangs over the world in its distorted, twisted imagery of pain and shame, not as a worldly power story, but as a story of love.
- How has an upside-down kingdom turned the world inside out?
- The secrets of this strange kingdom work in upside-down, unlikely, foolish ways because the God we meet in Jesus is unlike anything or anyone we've ever known.
- Powerful regimes usually change people from the outside in; but Jesus' influence changed people from the inside out.
- I have been mesmerized by the person of Jesus and the foolish nature of his power, and I remain so to this day.
- The cross is the very power of God made real in our lives.
- Will we live by the premises of the world or by the promises of his Word?
- The cross may have looked like losing, but it was winning.
- God created a new ecosystem: an ecosystem built on self-giving, an ecosystem that chose self-giving love over self-serving power.
- It is time to stop being compelled by the world's foolish power and instead to embrace, whatever it may cost our personal convenience and comfort, the powerful foolishness that is found in the cross of Jesus Christ, King of kings.

Chapter Two: Forsaken

- "My God, my God, why have you forsaken me?" is one of the most remarkable questions in the history of humanity.
- When God created the universe, he knew the cost of redeeming it. When he created human beings, he knew the cost of redeeming them.
- At some point in our lives we will find ourselves asking, "Why?" Or, more likely, shouting, screaming, or crying, *"Why?"*
- If God didn't withhold from us his very own Son, will God withhold anything we need?
- We can know that there is no situation or trouble that we will ever go through where Jesus isn't standing with us and cannot understand.
- The Holy Spirit is the life-giving Spirit, and he led Jesus through a life of ministry and healing and power to the place of sacrifice and suffering, to death and loss.
- The Spirit comforts us and cries: "There *is* possibility, there *is* hope, there *is* God even in the worst moments of your life!"
- You can know your future is secure and you are held firmly by Jesus, and once he grabs hold he never lets go.
- God is with you through divorce, he is with you through failure, he is with you through bereavement, through disappointment, through fear and guilt and shame.

Chapter Three: Finished

- We will never run out of grace or mercy; we will always be able to withdraw from the account that was settled by Christ on our behalf.

- "It is finished." Those three words give us the assurance that the bridge between humankind and God is intact.
- The blood of Jesus is the bridge to cross over into freedom and newness of life.
- Jesus can redeem [the past] and renew it, rebuilding and restoring us in the process and rewriting both my story and yours.
- Jesus' words on the cross—"It is finished"—sound as if they speak of an end, but could they actually signal a new beginning?
- There is always hope, even after we have said or felt that it is finished.

Chapter Four: Forgiven

- We can only be saved when we recognize Jesus for who he is, show our repentance, and ask for forgiveness.
- When we catch a glimpse of who Jesus truly is, when we get a sense of his relentless love, everything else fades into the background.
- The first person truly to understand what it is to be justified by faith in Jesus Christ alone was a robber on a cross.
- It was not nails but love that held God to a cross.
- At the cross there is the strangest and most beautiful encounter—a once-for-all meeting of human beings at their worst and God at his best.

Chapter Five: Friendship

- Regardless of gender, race, and nationality, the cross of Jesus is a message of hope for all who accept and put their faith in him.

- Friendship happens when mercy wins over justice.
- Jesus wants to use every single one of us to form this strange, upside-down kingdom where broken things are made whole.

Chapter Six: Freedom

- Our response to the cross is the real test of our spiritual condition.
- God's looking for complete honesty, vulnerability, and sincerity.
- You can either pretend to be perfect or you can repent. In my experience, it's one or the other. You can't do both.
- When truly set free, the people of God become extraordinary forces for good in the world.
- Christ knows the entire stories of your life and my life, and he wants to set us free from the hurts of the past to enable us to live in hope for the future.
- The power of the Spirit is unleashed with astonishing force through the apparent folly of the cross.

Chapter Seven: Forlorn

- The in-between God is a reality as much as the intervening God of Friday and Saturday.
- Where is God when we find ourselves sitting in the silent tomb of Saturday?
- No matter how dark and still the river looks or how frozen it becomes, in Christ there is always the power of resurrected life flowing beneath the depths.
- I know of no mature disciple of Christ who has not experienced the deep frustration of waiting for God to act.

- God may be silent, but he is not absent.
- When we sign up to a life of following Jesus, we have to accept that we will experience the glory of the resurrection as well as the burden of the crucifixion.
- For all of us there are Saturdays when all we have is the weight and the burden of taking the body of Christ onto our own frames.

Chapter Eight: Fulfilled

- This is a community empowered like no other then or since to change the world in which we live by being changed ourselves.
- Taken together, these three events—the cross, the resurrection, and the giving of the Holy Spirit—initiate and empower our agenda for change in the world.
- Jesus came to bring the kingdom of God to earth, to serve and not to be served, and "to give his life as a ransom for many" (Mark 10:45).
- Jesus did not die for some new religious philosophy or to make a point; he died *for us*.
- What Proverbs tells us is undoubtedly true: "What a person desires is unfailing love" (19:22).
- The cross is the decisive victory of God's way in the world, and the resurrection is the empowering victory—the first sign of this new era.
- What excites and motivates me is that the cross is a public act with liberating consequences for the whole of humanity.
- The power of the cross enables Christians in every sphere of life to demonstrate that the world can be different from the

prevailing narrative and indeed that it *is* different as a result of Christ's death.

- The cross is the core story of humanity, and it is the special calling of Christians to make this core story real in our everyday lives.
- Idol worship was replaced on the cross by the freedom to live in the light of a new relationship with the true God.
- The victory is the fact that the cross is the end of history. It marks the end of humanity's need to search for God. That defining quest, ongoing for millennia, has ended.
- We do not have an accuser but an advocate, one who took our punishment and paid the ultimate price with his own blood.
- Jesus rose again to underline that he had conquered the human delusion that death is the end.

Chapter Nine: Flourishing

- The cross started the regime change and the resurrection underwrote it, indicating that something new had been birthed.
- It is easy to forget that God loves and accepts us not because we are perfect but because of Jesus' perfect sacrifice, because of grace.
- Jesus met them not in a temple or a synagogue, but in their place of work, in their everyday routine, and there he sanctified their daily lives—and ours with theirs.
- Is it Facebook or Faithbook?
- What the cross secured, the resurrection cemented and the Spirit delivered: the power to bring about actual change.

- The resurrection underwrites this radical newness we now have. We are to live "for him who died [for us] and was raised again."
- The Spirit is not given to make us more spiritual but to make us fully human.
- God doesn't give us the Holy Spirit to let us put our feet up and wait for heaven.
- Pentecost empowers us to be restored in all four directions: with God, with self, with others, and with the world.
- This manifesto compels us to love the world, fractured as it is, and to commit ourselves to the task of fighting injustice—whether campaigning against modern-day slavery, or for the rights of the poor and marginalized, or for the well-being of the planet.
- Jesus knew his why. He knew where he came from and where he was going (John 8:14).
- We need to ask the Holy Spirit to awaken us to our core stories and to charge them with his power.
- We each can take our core story and plant it into Jesus' core story, the greatest one ever told—a narrative of love for us, our society, and the world.
- The Pope, one of the most influential people on the planet, has a core story: *people*.
- We have the power to partner with God to bring in his kingdom on a day-to-day basis and to live our lives from a place of acceptance and assurance that we will find our ultimate fulfillment in him.

NOTES

INTRODUCTION

1. Dietrich Bonhoeffer, *God Is on the Cross: Reflections on Lent and Easter* (Louisville, KY: Westminster John Knox Press, 2012), 69.
2. Brennan Manning, *The Importance of Being Foolish* (New York: HarperCollins, 2005), 160–61.
3. "And Can It Be That I Should Gain?" words by Charles Wesley, music by Thomas Campbell.

CHAPTER 1: FOOLISHNESS

1. Dave Eggers, *Your Fathers, Where Are They? And the Prophets, Do They Live Forever?* (New York: Knopf, 2014), 212, 36.
2. Ibid., 101.
3. Nwaocha Mind Ogechukwu, *The Secret Behind the Cross and Crucifix* (Strategic Book Publishing and Rights Agency, LLC, 2009), 52.
4. J. I. Packer, *Knowing God* (Downers Grove, IL: InterVarsity Press, 1973), 249.
5. N. T. Wright, "Christ the Power of God and the Wisdom of God," *NT Wright Page*, July 2, 2005, http://ntwrightpage.com/2016/03/29/christ-the-power-of-god-and-the-wisdom-of-god/.

CHAPTER 2: FORSAKEN

1. Timothy Keller, *Jesus the King: Understanding the Life and Death of the Son of God* (New York: Penguin, 2013), 6.
2. C. S. Lewis, *A Grief Observed* (New York: HarperCollins, 1961), 17–18.
3. Phillip Pullman, *The Golden Compass* (New York: Knopf, 1996), 213–14.
4. Ann Voskamp, *One Thousand Gifts: A Dare to Live Fully Right Where You Are* (Grand Rapids, MI: Zondervan, 2010), 154.
5. Timothy Keller, *Walking with God Through Pain and Suffering* (New York: Viking, 2013), 3.

CHAPTER 3: FINISHED

1. Christina Hoff Sommers, "Are We Living in a Moral Stone Age?" *Imprimis*, March 1998, vol. 27, no. 3, http://character-education.info /Articles/Sommers.pdf.
2. Francis Frangipane, *Strength for the Battle: Wisdom and Insight to Equip You for Spiritual Warfare* (Lake Mary, FL: Charisma House Book Group, 2017), 112.
3. Sheridan Voysey, *Resurrection Year* (Nashville: Thomas, 2013), xi, xii.

CHAPTER 4: FORGIVEN

1. Jayson Casper, "Forgiveness: Muslims Moved as Coptic Christians Do the Unimaginable, April 20, 2017, ChristianityToday.com, http://www.christianitytoday.com/news/2017/april/forgiveness -muslims-moved-coptic-christians-egypt-isis.html.
2. Fr. Boules George, St. Mark, Cleopatra (Cairo, Egypt), "A Message to Those Who Kill Us," http://www.copticdadandmom.com/fr -boules-george/.
3. Søren Kierkegaard, *The Portable Kierkegaard* (Canada: Emerald Knight Publishing, 2009), 161.
4. Ibid., 162.
5. Roland Herbert Bainton, *Here I Stand: A Life of Martin Luther* (Nashville: Abingdon Press, 1950), 39.

6. Philip Yancey, *Where Is God When It Hurts / What's So Amazing About Grace?* (Grand Rapids, MI: Zondervan, 2008), 348.

CHAPTER 5: FRIENDSHIP

1. Rick Warren, *The Purpose Driven Life*, Special Anniversary Edition (Grand Rapids, MI: Zondervan, 2012), 182.
2. Justin Welby, "Reconciliation Is Our 'Gift to the World': Archibishop Preaches in Guatemala," August 12, 2013, http://www.archbishop ofcanterbury.org/articles.php/5121/reconciliation-is-our-gift-to-the -world-archbishop-preaches-in-guatemala.
3. Ibid.
4. Peter Limb, *Nelson Mandela: A Biography* (Greenwood, 2008), 76.
5. Augustine, *Confessions*, trans. by Sarah Ruden (New York: Modern Library, 2017), 314.
6. Philip Yancey, *Where Is God When It Hurts / What's So Amazing About Grace?* (Grand Rapids, MI: Zondervan, 2008), 368.
7. N. T. Wright, *The Challenge of Jesus: Rediscovering Who Jesus Was and Is* (Downers Grove, IL: InterVarsity Press, 1998), 172.
8. My Modern Met Team, "Kintsugi: The Centuries-Old Art of Repairing Broken Pottery with Gold," *My Modern Met*, April 25, 2017, https://mymodernmet.com/kintsugi-kintsukuroi/.
9. Scott J. Jones and Bishop Bruce Ough, *The Future of the United Methodist Church* (Nashville: Abingdon Press, 2010), 64.
10. "What a Friend We Have in Jesus," words by Joseph Scriven, music by Charles Crozat Converse, public domain.

CHAPTER 6: FREEDOM

1. Famous D. L. Moody quote: https://books.google.co.uk/books.
2. John Calvin, *Commentary on Galatians and Ephesians*, William Pringle, trans., Christian Classics Ethereal Library, accessed October 22, 2015, http://www.ccel.org/ccel/calvin/calcom41.iii.iii.i.html.
3. Samuel Chadwick, *The Way to Pentecost* (Fort Washington, PA: CLC Publications, 2007), 22.

4. Lesslie Newbigin, *Foolishness to the Greeks: The Gospel and Western Culture* (London: SPCK, 1986), 150. See also pages 62–63 and 126 for other quotes.

CHAPTER 7: FORLORN

1. Alan E. Lewis, *Between Cross and Resurrection: A Theology of Holy Saturday* (Grand Rapids, MI: Wm. B. Eerdmans, 2001), 4.
2. Russel Moldovan, "Martin Luther King Jr." ChristianityToday.com, Christian History, issue 65, http://www.christianitytoday.com /history/issues/issue-65/martin-luther-king-jr.html.
3. Hans Urs von Balthasar, *Mysterium Pauschale: The Mystery of Easter* (2000), 110.
4. A. J. Swoboda, *A Glorious Dark: Finding Hope in the Tension Between Belief and Experience* (Grand Rapids, MI: Baker Books, 2014), 109.

CHAPTER 9: FLOURISHING

1. Brennan Manning, *Abba's Child: The Cry of the Heart for Intimate Belonging* (Colorado Springs: NavPress, 2015), 81.
2. Mark Zuckerberg, "Building Global Community," February 16, 2017, https://www.facebook.com/notes/mark-zuckerberg /building-global-community/10154544292806634/.
3. Allan D. Fitzgerald *Augustine Through the Ages: An Encyclopaedia*, 456.
4. John Anthony McGuckin, *The SCM Press A-Z of Patristic Theology* (2005), 213.
5. If you want to know more, read Rebecca Rischin's *For the End of Time: The Story of the Messiaen Quartet* (Ithaca, NY: Cornell University Press, 2006).

ABOUT THE AUTHOR

BORN AND RAISED IN SOUTH AFRICA, KEN COSTA studied law and philosophy at college in Johannesburg, where he was actively involved in the student protest movement against racial segregation in universities. In 1974 he moved to England to study law and theology at Cambridge University before joining the investment bank SG Warburg in the City of London. Over the next forty years, Ken continued to work in investment banking, becoming chairman of Europe, the Middle East, and Africa for UBS Investment Bank and later chairman of Lazard International. During this time Ken worked in mergers and acquisitions, advising global corporations on their international strategies, and in 2010 he played a key role in the sale of Harrods—perhaps the most famous department store in the world. In 2016, he was nominated as one of the City of London's top deal advisors of the last twenty years. His first book, *God at Work*, drew on this experience to explore what it means to live every day with purpose in the workplace. Ken also went on to make a series of short films called *God at Work Conversations*, which can be found at www.godatwork.org.uk/conversations.

He is also the author of *Know Your Why*, which deals with the purpose and identity of a generation grappling with unprecedented change. Ken says, "To know your why and to own your core story is the bravest thing anyone can do." www.knowyourwhybook.com/.

ABOUT THE AUTHOR

Besides his commercial work, Ken has spent much of his adult life involved in the leadership of Holy Trinity Brompton (HTB), the largest Anglican church in the United Kingdom, where he preaches regularly. He is dean of the HTB Leadership College London, which trains those in their twenties and thirties to be distinctive Christian leaders in their workplaces, and is also chairman emeritus of Alpha International—an evangelistic course born out of HTB, which he chaired for sixteen years and which has so far taught the basics of Christianity to an estimated 27 million people worldwide. He is chairman of Worship Central, a movement promoting worship events and courses across the globe. It was also at Cambridge that Ken got to know the current archbishop of Canterbury, Justin Welby, whose reconciliation and evangelism work he now supports as chairman of the Lambeth Trust and chairman of the Reconciling Leaders Network.

Given his professional experience, Ken has regularly been asked to speak on financial, ethical, and Christian issues at conferences and churches around the world. As emeritus professor of commerce at Gresham College London, he lectured on finance and ethics in the aftermath of the global financial crisis, and in 2011 he led the London Connection—an initiative seeking to encourage dialogue between the financiers in the City of London and the Occupy protesters who took up residence outside St Paul's Cathedral—at the request of the bishop of London. He was also a trustee of the Nelson Mandela UK Children's Fund for more than ten years, is currently fundraising patron for Great Ormond Street Children's Hospital, and was an advisory board member of the London Symphony Orchestra.

Ken is married to Dr. Fiona Costa, a classical musician and research fellow at the University of Roehampton, and they have four adult children.